SURVIVING 5 YEARS WITH RICE AND BEANS

DISCOVER THE 2 AMAZING BONUSES I HAVE IN STORE FOR YOU

Scan the QR Code or go to www.preppersurvivalbible.com/survival-guides for instant access to the 2 FREE life-saving guides that come with this Book:

BONUS #1 – BUSHCRAFT: How to survive 3 days in the wild | Be ready for critical days of emergency or crisis with fundamental techniques for food, water, and shelter

- how to find your bearings, food, and water; how to light a fire and survive for at least 3 days in the wild – even without equipment or supplies – if you suddenly need to leave your home.

BONUS #2 - THE PERFECT EMERGENCY BAG: The essential kit list for your Bug-Out bag | Get ready and pre-equipped for life-saving decisions when emergency strikes and you need to move fast

- a super-detailed list to prepare your perfect bug-out bag emergency kit, with all the essential tools you need to take with you to survive for weeks in case of a sudden emergency

100+ pages of practical and detailed information that you can apply right away even if you are a complete beginner.

Credits

Copyright 2022

All rights reserved.

This document is intended to provide accurate and reliable information regarding the subject matter. The publication is sold with the understanding that the publisher is not obligated to render qualified, officially permitted, or otherwise accountable services. If any advice is needed, whether legal or professional, it should be sought from a person experienced in the profession.

In no way is it lawful to reproduce, duplicate, or transmit any part of this document, whether by electronic means or in printed form. Recording of this publication is strictly prohibited, and any storage of this document is not permitted unless with the publisher's written permission.

TABLE OF CONTENTS

INTRODUCTION	9
CHAPTER 1. BREAKFAST	15
Salty Sandwich	16
Banana Smoothie	17
Waffle Sandwich With Honey and Red Berries	18
Oatmeal With Honey	19
Toast With Honey and Peanut or Almond Spread	19
Honey Banana With Walnuts	20
Banana Pancakes With a Couple of Incredible Ingredients	21
Keto Toast	23
Mint Green Smoothie	25
CHAPTER 2. LUNCH	27
Bean and Rice Burritos	28
Prepared Beans and Rice	30
Fried Rice With Vegetables	32
Rice Salad With Tuna, Broccoli, Cherry Tomatoes, and Corn	33
Rice With Pickled Chicken and Mushrooms	35
Rice Salad With Tomato and Pickled Tuna in Pickled Sauce	36
Beans With Clams	37
Hake With Beans and Mushrooms	38
Grilled Chicken Breast With Bean Puree	40
Mixed Salad With Canned Beans	41
Cuban Style Rice With Beans	42

Ground Beans	44
Bean Toast	45
Corned Beef Stew	47
Corned Beef Tacos	48
Easy Pea Risotto	49
Easy Baked Ham With Pineapple	50
Chickpea Curry	53
Bean and Rice Casserole	54
Traditional Recipe With a Mexican Twist	**56**
What Is Parboiled Rice?	**56**
Vegan Green Hummus	57
Grilled Venison	58
Chicken Fried Rice	59
Tuna Casserole in a Clay Pot	61
Chicken Salad Stuffed Avocado Recipe	62
CHAPTER 3. SOUPS	**65**
Pinto Bean and Rice Soup	66
Italian Soup	67
Bean Soup	68
White Bean Soup	69
Bean Noodle Soup With Pasta	70
White Rice Soup	72
Noodle Soup	73
Taco Soup	74
Tex-Mex Soup	75
Peanut Butter Soup	76
Black Bean Soup	78
Kale Soup	79

CHAPTER 4. DINNERS — 81

Beef Stew — 82
White Beans in Green Sauce — 83
Pressure Canned Venison — 84
Venison Medallions — 86
Roasted Deer — 87
Dried Meat — 88
Hardtack — 90
Cereal Bars — 91
Stir-Fried Vegetables — 92
Homemade Fried Tomato — 94
Chicken Soup — 95
Indian Stir-Fry — 96
Spicy Fried Chickpeas — 98

CHAPTER 5. SNACKS — 99

Rhubarb Cream — 100
Energy Bars — 101

CHAPTER 6. DESSERTS — 107

Green Pudding — 108
Lentil Candy Bars — 109
Lentils and Dates Brownies — 110
Homemade Ice Cream — 111
Tangerine Pudding — 111

CHAPTER 7. FRUITS AND VEGETABLES — 113

Marinated Grilled Tofu — 114
Avocado Green Salad — 116
Avocado Hummus — 118
Canned Cranberries — 119

Sautéed Green Vegetables	120
Avocado Cup Bread	121

CHAPTER 8. DRINKS AND OTHERS — 123

Sweet Rice Drink	124
Rice Milk With Chocolate	125
Rice Wine	126
Oatmeal	127
Other ways to eat oatmeal	128
Hard Candy	129

VARIOUS RECIPES THAT ARE QUICK TO MAKE — 131

Cold Brew Coffee	132
Overnight Oatmeal Porridge	132
Peanut and Chocolate Cookies	133
Macaroni Pot of the Forest	134
Couscous With Chickpeas and Pesto	134
Mexican Burrito With Beans and Peppers	135
Red Lentil Dahl	136
Rice Noodles With Coconut Milk and Tofu	136
Buckwheat Bowl	137
Hummus Without a Food Processor	138

CONCLUSION — 139

INTRODUCTION

What would you eat if grocery stores were not an option?

How would you cook without gas and electricity?

How would you preserve your food without a refrigerator and freezer?

If you are like most people, you would probably answer something like:

"Why should I worry when I can just buy everything I need?"

But If you think like millions of Americans, then you are already prepping for the not-too-distant future when the collapse of our economy or a catastrophic event could obliterate our present lifestyle forever.

Obviously, two things that would radically change following an economic collapse, war, or the failure of the electricity grid, are your diet and the way you cook your food.

So, many preppers experiment with how food was stored and cooked back in the days of the great pioneers – when cooking on open fires was quite unlike today's cooking with microwave ovens or electric stoves.

And back then, in the days of the pioneers, the recipes were simple.

There were no specialty stores full of hard-to-find ingredients or hard-to-preserve foods.

Most of them could only rely on their own food stocks. Some lucky ones had access to milk and eggs. But most didn't.

Even when the pioneers stayed in one place for a few months, they needed to be able to cope with all kinds of risk.

Just think that a single storm could wipe out all their food supplies.

Of course, there were no refrigerators, and even canning was not always possible because it would involve having the jars to do so, so nothing was wasted.

Dry bread turned into bread pudding. A bone turned into a soup.

Ingredients were scarce.

As a result, most of their recipes were based on a few essential ingredients.

As you can imagine, feeding your family wasn't easy.

Procuring and storing food were constant concerns, both physically and mentally.

Especially during the long, cold and deadly winter months.

Traveling thousands of kilometers on the trails of the West or suffering in the wilderness in the coldest months of the year led to desperate people eating oxen, horses and pets ...

... or dying of thirst or contaminated water ...

... not to mention poisoning from toxic cow's milk.

Despite these enormous difficulties, the pioneer women carried with them their own collection of recipes, the memory of the security left behind and the hope of new abundance in the future.

Now you could probably ask me:

"Why are you telling me all this?"

You see, the experiences I have gained often lead me to compare the lifestyle of the great American pioneers with that of people affected by a severe sudden crisis.

The fact is, the pioneers were tough.

And these days we are the opposite, we are used to our conveniences and comforts, and a crisis situation would catch the vast majority of people unprepared.

Think about it for a moment.

If an event catapults you from one day to the next into a situation similar to the pioneers' – no electricity, no running water, no supermarkets – then you too have to know how to preserve and cook food… starting from scratch.

The truth is that in order to cope for any length of time in a survival situation, you need to know how to cook food and prepare meals with quick decisions and very few options available…

If you're only just beginning to approach the world of preppers right now, you may well think that long-life foods are boring, and recipes pretty bland.

The good news is that you won't need to compromise on taste…

… thanks to the delicious recipes that I am happy to share with you.

Here's what you'll find in this manual:

- Mouthwatering recipes, simple to prepare, even without electricity, running water or supermarkets at hand
- Ingredients that are healthy and easy to find in nature. And no, you don't have to be a hunting and fishing expert
- Creative and tasty combinations: you don't need to compromise on flavor even with long life preserved food
- Recipes designed for fire pot cooking, like in the great pioneer days, and completely different from microwave or electric stove versions

- Lots of recipes for indulgent desserts. Including those that you can prepare even if you don't have access to milk or eggs
- Appetizing recipes for all tastes, also vegan, vegetarian and gluten-free to help you accommodate any food intolerances

If you too want to learn how to cook lots of delicious recipes with simple, healthy, and readily available ingredients…

… even without supermarkets, refrigerators, freezers, electricity, gas, internet, and all of today's usual amenities…

… then take some time out for yourself, read this book and start experimenting with your new crisis-proof way of cooking.

And the best part is that most of these recipes will surprise you.

Give them a try and enjoy your tasty results!

CHAPTER 1
BREAKFAST

These are some of the breakfasts that you could prepare with what you have available in your bunker. Some great ideas that you could also adapt according to your stored foods at home, for yourself and your family to enjoy.

Salty Sandwich

Ingredients

- 160 g (5.6 oz) pickled or canned tuna
- 75 ml mayonnaise
- 75 ml fresh coriander
- 50 g (1.7 oz) purple onion
- 50 g (1.7 oz) red pepper
- 2 capers
- 2 teaspoons lemon juice
- Salt
- Ground black pepper
- 2 bread slices

Method of preparation

1. Start by chopping all the vegetables and mixing them in a bowl with the tuna, capers, and mayonnaise.
2. Taste the mixture and add salt and pepper if required. The tuna itself is already slightly salty, so just be aware when adding extra.
3. After this, you can spread it on two slices of bread of your choice.
4. In the bowl, place the lemon juice, cilantro, peppers, and the rest of the ingredients. Add this mixture to the bread and enjoy.

Banana Smoothie

A banana smoothie can be prepared with a hand blender if you don't have electricity so that you can feed yourself and your family. Bananas contain potassium and are a good source of energy.

Ingredients

- 2 tbsp sugar
- 2 cups milk, if you have it
- 1 banana
- If you have electricity, you can add ice

Method of preparation

1. Peel the bananas and cut them into small pieces. Put them in a blender or a high-walled container to handle everything.
2. Add sugar, milk, and a little crushed ice, if you can, so that the smoothie is cold.
3. Blend well until all ingredients are combined.
4. Serve in a glass or preferably in a cup, and if you want to give it that final touch, place a slice of banana on the rim of the glass.

Bonus: If you want to go from a premium banana smoothie to a MEGA banana smoothie just for the sweet tooth, you can add a spoonful of dulce de leche or peanut butter to the mix.

Banana smoothies are great on their own or with your cookies, and you get a complete breakfast. Another excellent way to give it a different touch is to add slices of other fruits during the preparation process or keep the smoothie in the refrigerator for a while to make it firmer and colder.

Waffle Sandwich With Honey and Red Berries

This is a delicious breakfast where you combine red fruits and honey.

Ingredients

- 2 whole-grain waffles
- 1/4 tbsp butter
- 1/2 cup berries
- 1/4 cup honey

Method of preparation

1. Blend or mash ½ cup of berries. Set aside.
2. Melt butter in a saucepan over medium heat.
3. Add honey and bring to a boil. Simmer over low heat for 2 to 3 minutes.
4. Add the berry puree and simmer for another 2–3 minutes, until the syrup thickens slightly. Set the honey syrup aside and keep it warm.
5. Arrange the two waffles on a plate. Top the waffles with ¼ cup of fresh berries.
6. Add 1/4 of the syrup and top with another waffle.

Oatmeal With Honey

This is a delicious recipe made with oatmeal and honey that will certainly set you up for the day.

Ingredients

- 1 tbsp chopped walnuts
- 1/2 tbsp cinnamon
- 1 cup of water
- 1/2 cup traditional oatmeal
- 1 tsp honey

Method of preparation

1. Boil water in a pot and add the oatmeal. Stir until cooked, approximately 5 minutes.
2. Add honey, cinnamon, and walnuts. Stir well and serve.

Toast With Honey and Peanut or Almond Spread

This toast will nourish you, and it will also provide you with a good boost of energy and nutritional benefits.

Ingredients

- 2 tbsp almond or peanut cream
- 2 slices low salt sprouted wheat or whole wheat bread
- 2 tbsp honey

Method of preparation

1. Spread two slices of toasted bread with peanut or almond butter.
2. Add 1 teaspoon of honey to each slice and serve.

Honey Banana With Walnuts

The banana itself is already nutritious, but you will have a delicious combination if you add a touch of walnuts and honey.

Ingredients

- 1 tbsp peanut butter
- 1/2 banana
- 1 tsp honey
- Walnuts

Method of preparation

1. Cut the banana vertically.
2. Mix the peanut butter and honey until you get a consistent mixture. Add the walnuts.
3. Spread the mixture inside the bananas and press down.

Banana Pancakes With a Couple of Incredible Ingredients

This recipe is high in calories and nutritious, so it will help you stay well-fueled. You can make it with oatmeal and lots of fruit; it's a great start to the day.

Ingredients

- 1 large ripe banana
- 2 eggs
- A pinch of salt
- Sodium bicarbonate or chemical yeast
- Cinnamon powder
- 1/2 tsp pure unsweetened cocoa
- 1 tsp brown sugar
- Virgin olive oil
- Fruit pieces

Method of preparation

1. Peel the bananas, chop them and mash them with a fork until they have a mush consistency, even with a few lumps; it is better if it is cooked and soft. Then, beat two eggs with a whisk and pour over the bananas. Mix well with a large spoon until you have a uniform batter.
2. To this mix, add the sodium bicarbonate or chemical yeast, cinnamon powder, unsweetened cocoa, and brown sugar. Mix once again.
3. Heat a non-stick pan over a medium fire and lightly grease

with butter or neutral oil. Pour the batter with the help of a spoon or measuring cup and pour the amount into about 6–8 small or medium pancakes, between 7 and 10 cm in diameter. It is better not to cook too many at the same time.

4. Leave in the pan for 2–4 minutes, or until the edges can be easily lifted without sticking. It is best to check them lightly with a good thin non-stick spatula, to check that it is cooked. Flip them over and cook for a few more minutes.

5. Remove the pancakes while they are still cooking and cover them with a cloth or cling film to keep them warm, or if you bake them, you can take advantage of the residual heat from the oven. They are also good if you let them cool and then heat them for a few minutes in the microwave.

6. If you want, you can add extra ingredients to the batter, for example, small pieces of fresh fruit while the pancakes are cooking.

Keto Toast

These toasts are simple but very nutritious and can be made with whatever you have in the bunker.

Ingredients

For the cup of bread

- 2 tbsp cream
- 3 tbsp egg powder
- A pinch of salt
- 1 1/2 tbsp baking powder
- 2 tbsp almonds
- 1 tsp of butter

For the creamy mixture

- 2 tbsp butter
- A pinch of salt
- 1/2 tsp ground cinnamon
- 2 tbsp whipping cream
- 3 tbsp powdered egg

Method of preparation

For the cup of bread

1. Butter a large bowl or shallow dish.
2. Add all the dry ingredients to make the bread and mix

with a fork or spoon. Add the eggs and cream. Mix until you obtain a uniform consistency without lumps.
3. Microwave on high power (about 700 watts) for 2 minutes. Check that the bread is done in the center. If not, cook for another 15–30 seconds.
4. Let the bread cool and remove it from the bowl. Cut in half.

For the creamy mixture

1. In a bowl or deep dish, combine the eggs, cream, and cinnamon with a pinch of salt.
2. Pour the cream mixture over the bread slices and let them soak well. Turn them over several times so that the slices absorb as much of the egg mixture as possible.
3. Fry in butter and serve immediately.
4. This recipe is based on our low-carb cup bread, but you can use any other type of low-carb bread you like.
5. If you don't want to weigh the dry ingredients, you can prepare the baking mix ahead of time. You will need 10 tablespoons (66 grams) of almond flour, 10 tablespoons (72 grams) of coconut flour, 1 teaspoon of salt, and 2 1/2 teaspoons of baking powder. This will give you a prepared mixture that yields 10 servings.

Mint Green Smoothie

This delicious green juice will provide your body with the necessary fiber it needs and will leave you feeling full.

Ingredients

- A cucumber, which has a lot of water and is delicious.
- Apple, choose those that are not sweet, such as green apples.
- Celery, with a bitter taste and intense aroma, with vegetable proteins and antioxidants.
- Lemon is alkalizing, refreshing, and contains a lot of vitamin C.
- Spinach is nutritious and low in calories.
- Mint leaves, give freshness and aroma to any drink or juice.

Method of preparation

1. Preparing this green juice couldn't be easier. You'll see how it only takes a minute.
2. Start by washing all the fruits and vegetables. Remember, leave all the skin and leaves on because that's where most of your vitamins and minerals are found.
3. Then place all the ingredients in a blender or juicer. When ready, pour the juice into a glass and add 1 or 2 ice cubes if available.
4. That's it! Enjoy the juice.

CHAPTER 2
LUNCH

These lunches can be made with canned goods, pickles, preserves, and everything you have learned to store in the previous books. You can make them your way or even combine them with what you have. Hopefully, this section will give you some great ideas for tasty and nutritional lunches for your family.

You will also see that lunch doesn't have to be boring and unappetizing when you are in the confines of your shelter.

Bean and Rice Burritos

These *burritos* will fill you up with lots of nutrients, and you can make them with canned, preserved food, or the rice you have in your storeroom.

Ingredients

- 3 tbsp chili powder
- 2 chopped garlic
- 1 chopped onion
- 2 tsp vegetable oil
- 1 cup of rice
- 1 can of red and green bell peppers
- 1 can of black beans
- 1/2 tsp ground cumin
- 8 (8-inch) flour tortillas
- 2 thinly sliced onions
- 1 cup grated cheese, if you have it
- 1/2 cup light sour cream
- 1/2 cup salsa

Method of preparation

1. In a large skillet, heat the oil over a medium-high fire. Add the onion, garlic, paprika, and cumin when hot enough. Sauté for 3 to 5 minutes or until the onions are soft.
2. Add the rice, black beans, and corn and cook over a medium heat, stirring frequently. This process may take about 3 minutes or until the mixture is heated through. Remove from heat.

3. Spoon ½ cup of the rice mixture into the center of each *tortilla*. Top each with 2 tablespoons of cheese, 1 tablespoon of green onion, and 2 teaspoons of sour cream. Then roll up and add a spoonful of salsa just before serving.

Tip: Squeeze fresh lime over the *burrito* for extra flavor and freshness.

We love *burritos*

In case you're still hesitating… YES! Rice is one of the main ingredients in a true burrito. Rice has a special role in this recipe because it is an excellent ingredient in any preparation. This burrito is prepared with your rice, with no effort in the kitchen, and without sacrificing any flavor; this dish is a whole-grain dish. It's ideal when you crave a hearty and delicious home-cooked meal. You'll be happy to know that most of the ingredients you'll need to make this burrito are products you'll never be without in your pantry.

This recipe is meant for those days when you don't have a lot of time, so I recommend using canned vegetables and beans. You can prepare your black beans and chop fresh vegetables if you wish. However, don't forget to sauté the vegetables with the seasoning for a more flavorful *burrito* filling.

Prepared Beans and Rice

A complete lunch like this one will give you what you need to be fully nourished. It is easy to make.

Ingredients

- 5 artichokes
- Bay leaves
- 1 sweet paprika.
- 60 ml crushed tomato
- 1 medium red bell pepper
- 3 garlic cloves
- 2 spring onions
- 250 g (8.8 oz) thin white beans
- Salt
- Sherry vinegar
- 4 handfuls of round rice

Method of preparation

1. Drain the soaked beans, rinse them lightly and cook them with plenty of cold water, a shallot, and a peeled clove of garlic. Pour cold water over them while boiling two or three times. The time depends on the type of beans and water, about 60–90 minutes, or just 15–17 minutes in a crockpot.
2. Chop another onion and garlic. Peel and dice the red peppers with a vegetable peeler, discarding the seeds. Heat one tablespoon of oil in a frying pan and sauté the onion

with the garlic and a pinch of salt until transparent.
3. Add the pepper and fry for a few minutes, then add the chili powder and stir quickly over a low heat to prevent it from burning. Add the tomatoes and bay leaves, stir and lower the heat to the minimum to make the sauce while you peel the artichokes.
4. Remove the artichoke's core by removing the tough outer leaves, cutting off the tips, and peeling the stems. When wiping each unit with lemon, do so generously to prevent them from oxidizing. Cut into quarters and add a pinch of salt to the pan.
5. Sauté everything for a few minutes, then carefully add the cooked beans. Stir, add vinegar, and cover with broth or water. Cook for about 5–8 minutes, then add a handful of rice. Continue heating over medium fire until cooked through and the artichokes are done.
6. If necessary, check the liquid level to add more broth or water to maintain flavor consistency. It will thicken as it cools. Remove bay leaves, taste, and add salt and pepper as required. They will taste richer as they cool.

Fried Rice With Vegetables

Fried rice is very delicious, and with this recipe, you will be able to make it easily and have it available for your family to enjoy.

Ingredients

- Salt
- Olive oil
- 1/2 tsp powdered ginger
- 1 tsp oyster sauce, if you have it
- 4 tbsp soy sauce
- 90 g (3.17 oz) freezer peas
- 4 large mushrooms
- 1 carrot
- 1 red bell pepper
- 1/2 onion
- 250 g (8.8 oz) rice.

Method of preparation

1. Start by cooking the rice in a pot with plenty of boiling water and a pinch of salt.
2. Once the rice is cooked, remove it from heat, drain the rice, and reserve it for later use.
3. While the rice is cooking, wash the mushrooms and cut them into small pieces.
4. Peel the onions and carrots, wash the red peppers and chop all the vegetables.

5. Heat a few tablespoons of olive oil in a frying pan over a medium flame and fry the chopped vegetables (including the mushrooms) for about 5–6 minutes, until tender.
6. Add the frozen peas and sauté for another 4–5 minutes.
7. Pour in soy sauce, and oyster sauce, add ginger powder and stir until combined.
8. Add the well-drained rice, mix everything and cook over medium heat for another 4–5 minutes, stirring occasionally.
9. If necessary, add a little salt to the fried vegetable rice. Serve warm.

Rice Salad With Tuna, Broccoli, Cherry Tomatoes, and Corn

This is a salad that you can prepare either with canned or fresh ingredients that you have grown in your garden. You will see how you will be able to prepare many simple and quick recipes with what you have available in your house.

Ingredients

- Pepper
- Salt
- Olive oil
- 1 lime
- 200 g (7 oz) canned tuna
- 12 tomatoes

- 300 g (10.5 oz) broccoli
- 1 jar of corn
- 1 tsp salt
- 1-liter water
- 300 g (10.5 oz) rice

Method of preparation

1. For the rice, bring one liter of water to a boil and add salt
2. Divide the broccoli into florets; wash, dry, and chop the cherry tomatoes. Then open and drain the canned corn.
3. Add the broccoli and rice, cook, drain and set aside to cool.
4. For the balsamic vinegar, mix the salt, lime juice, and oil in a bowl.
5. Add the cold rice, broccoli, cherry tomatoes, tuna, and corn to a salad bowl.
6. Add the balsamic vinegar, toss to combine, and serve the salad, finishing with freshly ground pepper.

Rice With Pickled Chicken and Mushrooms

Rice goes with almost anything, and preserves are a great companion for this universal grain in every diet worldwide. Add a marinated chicken sauce or a mushroom sauce to the rice that you cook, with a little garlic and onion to serve. It's a quick and easy dish that will be finger-licking good.

Ingredients

- Chinese onion
- Bay leaf
- Olive oil
- 200 g (7 oz) canned mushrooms
- A dash of poultry stock
- A drizzle of white wine, if you have it
- 3 garlic cloves
- 1 onion
- 1 can pickled chicken
- 500 ml round grain rice

Method of preparation

1. Place one tablespoon of oil in a frying pan. Heat and sauté a whole garlic clove, including the skin.
2. Place the rice in the saucepan, add one teaspoon of salt and stir until the rice is impregnated with the oil.
3. Add 4 cups of water and heat over a high flame. When it starts to boil, lower the heat, add a bay leaf and cook for 20 minutes.

4. Remove the chicken from the container and shred it, removing the bones, if any.
5. Peel and chop the onion and garlic and cook them in a pan with oil.
6. Add the mushrooms and sauté for a few minutes.
7. Add the wine and broth and let reduce.
8. Add the chicken and cook everything together for a few minutes.
9. Serve the rice on a plate, place the chicken on top and garnish with chopped chives.

Rice Salad With Tomato and Pickled Tuna in Pickled Sauce

For summertime, I recommend this rice salad with tomato and pickled tuna; you will see that it is delicious.

Ingredients

- Olive oil to taste
- 1 piece of tuna
- 2 cups of rice
- 1 green pepper
- 1 tomato

Method of preparation

1. If you have electricity, cook the rice in the normal way, or prepare the precooked rice in the microwave according to the manufacturer's instructions. Allow it to cool.

2. Cut the tomatoes into cubes.
3. Cut a piece of green bell pepper.
4. Combine the ingredients with the marinated tuna.
5. Add a little extra virgin olive oil. Do not use vinegar so you can appreciate all the flavors of the marinade.
6. Serve in individual bowls and enjoy.

Beans With Clams

This is a very nutritious and low-fat recipe because clams are rich in essential minerals (iron, phosphorus, potassium, calcium) and vitamin B. In addition, they contain high amounts of omega 3, whose consumption is associated with the regulation of blood cholesterol levels.

Ingredients

- Salt, parsley, and pepper
- 125 ml white wine
- Olive oil
- 1 garlic clove
- 1 ripe tomato
- 2 onions
- Canned clams
- 1 can of beans

Method of preparation

1. First, peel and julienne the onion.
2. Heat the oil in a skillet over a medium fire and add the onion and chopped garlic. Fry for a few minutes.
3. When the onions are transparent add the ripe tomatoes that you peeled and diced earlier.
4. Next, wash the clams and add them to the sauce and the white wine.
5. When the clams are open, add a can of beans and adjust the water according to your desired texture.
6. Add salt, pepper, and parsley, and finally simmer for about 20 minutes.
7. Now you have your clams ready for you to enjoy!

Hake With Beans and Mushrooms

This is a quick, easy, and very nutritious recipe that contains white fish, beans, and vegetables of high nutritional value and low in fat.

Ingredients

- Salt and pepper
- Olive oil
- Walnuts
- 1 garlic clove
- ½ onion

- Mushrooms
- Chard
- 1 can of beans
- Canned hake
- Soy sauce.
- Turmeric

Method of preparation

1. First, pour a few tablespoons of extra virgin olive oil into a frying pan and cook the hake. Set aside.
2. Place the previously washed and shredded mushrooms and onion, and the garlic cloves in the same pan.
3. When everything is cooked, add the beets and spices to taste.
4. Then, wash and drain the beans and add them to the pot.
5. Simmer for a few minutes so that all the flavors come together.
6. Finally, put the corresponding portion on a plate and add chopped walnuts and some soft cheese to garnish.

Grilled Chicken Breast With Bean Puree

Here's a complete recipe to serve as lunch or dinner without resorting to convenience or ultra-processed foods. In addition, it can be adapted for vegetarians by substituting chicken breasts for tofu.

Ingredients

- Salt, pepper, and oregano
- Olive oil
- Lemon juice
- 2 garlic cloves
- 1 onion
- 1 red bell pepper
- Canned chicken breast
- 1 can of beans

Method of preparation

1. First, remove the beans from the container and rinse them with the help of a colander.
2. Heat the oil in a frying pan over medium fire and add the peeled onion, chopped garlic, peppers, and the beans you cut earlier.
3. Then sauté for a few minutes and blend with the help of a hand blender until a uniform texture is obtained.
4. Add the juice of one lemon, salt, pepper, oregano, and extra virgin olive oil. Set aside.
5. Then, heat a little oil in a frying pan over a high fire and sauté the previously sliced chicken breast until fragrant.

6. To serve this meal, start by putting a few spoonfuls of mashed vegetables and beans in the bottom of a deep dish and adding the chicken strips. You can garnish with chopped nuts or olive oil, and mint leaves to finish.

Mixed Salad With Canned Beans

Without a doubt, salad is the simplest recipe when it comes to using a can of beans. Here we come up with a recipe using hard-boiled eggs and tuna—simply delicious!

Ingredients

- Salt and garlic powder
- Vinegar
- Olive oil
- 2 cans of sweet corn
- 1 red bell pepper
- 1 onion
- 3 cans of tuna
- 3 boiled eggs
- Olives
- 1 can of beans

Method of preparation

1. This recipe is very easy to make. Peel and dice all the ingredients, then add them to a bowl with the washed and drained vegetables. Season with oil, salt, and vinegar and it's ready to eat.

Cuban Style Rice With Beans

This rice will be delicious, and you will be able to make it in a very short time with a few ingredients that will fill your recipe with flavor.

Ingredients

- Olive oil
- Vinegar
- Sugar
- ½ tsp paprika
- 1 tsp dried oregano
- 1 bay leaf
- ½ an onion
- 3 garlic cloves
- 100 g (3.52 oz) green bell pepper
- 225 g (7.93 oz) black beans
- 225 g (7.93 oz) rice

Method of preparation

1. Soak the beans in a bowl with water for 12 hours. You can keep them overnight. After soaking, drain and set aside.

2. Wash the peppers and cut them into small cubes. Peel the garlic and onion and cut them into small pieces as well.
3. Pour 1 liter of water into a saucepan. Add half of the pepper, half of the onion, half of the garlic, the bay leaves, and the soaked and drained beans. Cover the pot and cook over

medium/low heat for 45 minutes from the time the water begins to boil.

How to make the *sofrito* vegetables and final cooking

1. While the beans are cooking, prepare the sauce with the rest of the vegetables. In a frying pan, heat the olive oil. Then, add the onion, bell pepper, and remaining garlic.
2. Sauté the vegetables until soft. Add the cumin, oregano, and paprika. Stir well and cook for 1–2 minutes so that the flavors combine well. Remove from heat.
3. When the beans have cooked for 45 minutes, add the sautéed vegetables and a pinch of salt to the pot. Cover the pot again and continue cooking the beans for a further 30 minutes.
4. After this time, add the vinegar and sugar and continue cooking for 15 minutes. If you see that there is too much liquid left, you can cook the last part uncovered. You can also mash one tablespoon of beans to help them thicken.

Preparing the rice and the final presentation

1. While the beans are finishing cooking, you will prepare the rice. Start by heating a pot and adding the rice, a pinch of salt, and water. Cook the rice for 18 minutes.
2. Serve the beans along with the freshly cooked rice. You can accompany this dish with traditional fried plantain and some cilantro leaves.

Ground Beans

Since you probably have a good supply of beans at home, you will be able to enjoy preparing this recipe, and I'm sure you are going to like it.

Ingredients

- 2 tbsp oil
- 1 tbsp cumin
- 1 fresh thyme
- 1 stalk celery
- 1 onion
- 2 small or medium tomatoes
- 2 sweet chilies
- 3 sprigs of cilantro
- 5 garlic cloves
- 250 ml evaporated milk
- 1/2 k (1.1 lb.) black or red beans
- Salt and water

Method of preparation

1. Wash the beans and let them soak in water for at least 6 to 8 hours (one night before is fine), then drain the water and rewash the beans.
2. After washing them, put them in the pressure cooker and cook for 20 to 30 minutes.
3. After the beans have boiled, drain them, always keeping a little of the remaining broth, and mix them with a little

water until you get a creamy consistency. Then return it to the fire and finally to the oven for a few more minutes.
4. Meanwhile, chop the onion and garlic and transfer them to the pan. Sauté until it crystallizes, then add the chopped tomatoes, garlic, chili, and celery. Let them cook in their juices.
5. When everything is ready, add the bean cream to the sauce and season with salt and pepper.
6. Let them simmer for a few minutes, constantly stirring a little at a time until they are completely mixed.
7. When ready, remove from heat and serve with grated cheese or some tostadas.

I recommend this recipe for lunch, mainly because it is easy to make. That's the great thing about beans: they have a variety of uses and are easy to prepare. You can accompany this recipe with some delicious tacos or bread.

Bean Toast

With beans, you can also make toast. Here's how to do it:

Ingredients

This is what you need for the toast:

- 1 tbsp vegetable oil
- 1 tbsp chili chipotle
- 1 cup refried beans
- Corn toast

For the decoration you need:

- ¼ lettuce
- 1 cup of cream
- 1 ½ cup queso fresco
- 2 tomatoes
- 1 avocado
- ½ onion
- 2 sprigs of cilantro
- Sauce if you wish

Method of preparation

1. Finely chop the lettuce and the cilantro.
2. Cut the onions and tomatoes into half-moon shapes. Scoop out all the avocado pulp and add it with the cheese in a bowl.
3. In a frying pan, pour oil with the beans and add the chili chipotle, and sauté; add a pinch of salt and pepper, and cook for at least 5 minutes.
4. Then, after the beans are cooked, you must put them on a toast and add lettuce, tomato, onion, and avocado and sprinkle with cheese and red sauce. This delicious toast is ready to serve.

Corned Beef Stew

While you're in your confinement, you'll never eat anything as good as this recipe I'll show you below:

Ingredients

- 2 tbsp olive oil
- 6 medium potatoes, peeled
- 1 medium onion sliced
- 2 garlic cloves
- 2 cans pastrami
- ¾ of a bag of frozen green peas
- 5 tbsp mayonnaise
- 1 tbsp salsa

Method of preparation

1. Put the potatoes in a large pot and fill it with water; bring it to a boil over a high heat. Reduce heat to a simmer and cook for about 15 minutes until the potatoes are tender. Drain and set aside.
2. Heat the oil in a large saucepan over a medium fire and cook the onions, occasionally stirring, until tender, for about 5 minutes. Add the potatoes and cook, stirring gently, until crisp, for about 8 minutes. Add garlic and cook for 30 seconds.
3. Add the cans of pastrami and mix with the remaining ingredients until combined. Cook, occasionally stirring, until the mixture is thoroughly heated through, about 5 minutes. Serve with fried eggs if desired.

Corned Beef Tacos

I have some delicious tacos that you're going to love:

Ingredients

- 8 corn tortillas
- 1 (25-ounce) can of corned beef stew
- 1 tbsp vegetable oil

Method of preparation

1. Heat the vegetable oil in a large saucepan over a medium fire.
2. Open the can of corned beef and place the meat in the pan with the oil. Spread the meat with a spatula.
3. Cook for about 15 minutes, frequently stirring to cook evenly.
4. Heat the tortillas over the direct fire.
5. Place the cooked corned beef in the center of each tortilla.
6. Serve and enjoy!

Easy Pea Risotto

Peas will never taste the same again after you've eaten this risotto.

Ingredients

- ½ cup Parmesan cheese
- 2 tbsp rice
- 1 tbsp olive oil
- 1 lb. peas
- 2 ¼ cups of water
- 1 can of chicken broth

Method of preparation

1. In a 2-quart covered saucepan, heat the chicken broth and 2 1/4 cups of water over a high fire until boiling.
2. Meanwhile, in a large microwave-safe bowl, place peas and 2 tablespoons of water; cover with airtight plastic wrap and microwave for 4 minutes. In a blender, combine 1 1/2 cup of peas and 1/4 cup of the hot broth mixture.
3. Remove the center part of the blender lid; cover with a cloth and puree the pea and broth mixture. Set the remaining peas aside.
4. Combine the olive oil and rice in a 3 1/2- to a 4-quart microwave-safe bowl. Cook, uncovered, in the microwave for 1 minute on high. Add the remaining hot broth mixture; cover the bowl with aerated plastic wrap and microwave on medium (50% power) for 10 minutes, stirring once during cooking.

5. Add pea puree; cover with aerated plastic wrap and cook on medium heat (50% power) for another 8 minutes or until most of the liquid is absorbed. Stir in Parmesan cheese, 1/4 teaspoon of salt, 1/4 teaspoon of freshly ground black pepper, and the remaining peas.
6. To serve, ladle risotto into 4 shallow bowls and garnish with grated Parmesan cheese.

Easy Baked Ham With Pineapple

Canned ham is a versatile and convenient ingredient when you need a light meal that can feed many people. Fully cooked vacuum-packed ham can be seasoned with various spices and other ingredients such as vegetables, root vegetables, or fruits. Our classic combination of pineapple rings and smoked and salted ham is a beautiful centerpiece, that is delicious, economical, and easy to prepare.

Although canned ham's flavor and texture are inferior to fresh ham, it has a big advantage in terms of storage stability. Having a can of ham in your pantry allows you to make a hearty meal at the last minute. In general, a family-size can of ham may last up to two years in the pantry. However, read labels carefully, as some brands require keeping them in the refrigerator.

Serve ham with pineapple, baked or mashed potatoes, and a salad for a hearty meal you can sit down and enjoy without sweating in the kitchen. Before you begin, be sure to have kitchen twine and toothpicks on hand.

Ingredients

- 1 1/2 tbsp water
- 1 tbsp cornstarch
- 1 tbsp chili powder
- 1 tbsp salsa
- 2 tbsp lemon juice
- 1/4 cup brown sugar
- 1/2 cup chili sauce
- 1 (20-ounce) can of pineapple that is in rings if you have available
- 3 pounds canned ham

Method of preparation

1. Gather the ingredients.
2. Preheat the oven to 325ºF. With a very sharp knife, cut the ham into 1/2-inch-thick slices, almost all the way through, but not quite.
3. Tie the ham around the perimeter with a piece of kitchen twine to hold the ham in place.
4. Drain the canned pineapple, reserving 1/4 cup of syrup.
5. Combine the pineapple syrup with the chili paste, brown sugar, lime juice, salsa, and chili powder in a bowl. Set aside.
6. Place the ham on the baking sheet or baking sheet rack.
7. Place the pineapple slices around the ham, securing with toothpicks.

8. Pour the reserved sweet and sour sauce over the entire ham.
9. Bake the entire piece in the preheated oven for 1 1/2 hours, often basting with sauce.
10. After the baking time has elapsed, place the ham on a plate, remove the string and replace the pineapple slices around it.
11. Cover the ham loosely with aluminum foil to keep it warm.

Now it's time to make the sauce:

1. Pour the juices from the pan into a 2-cup measuring cup and place enough hot water if necessary to make 1 1/4 cups of total liquid. Transfer to a small saucepan.
2. Combine cornstarch and cold water in a small bowl and whisk until smooth.
3. Add the cornstarch mixture to the saucepan and the pan juices and cook over a medium heat, stirring, until thickened and bubbling.
4. Drizzle some of the sauce over the ham and pineapple.
5. Set the remaining sauce aside.

How Can I Reuse the Leftover Ham?

Store the leftover ham in the refrigerator and enjoy it for the next three to five days. If you don't have the opportunity to eat it right away, freeze it for up to two months. Here are some ideas on how to use leftover ham in other delicious dishes:

1. Fry leftover ham slices and serve with rice and beans or baked potatoes and vegetables.
2. Make mashed potatoes with chopped ham and serve with fried eggs.
3. Mix ham chunks with baked or mashed potatoes. Add bacon cubes, shredded mozzarella, and heavy cream. Bake at 375ºF until the top is crisp.
4. Top your favorite potato or pasta salad with ham chunks.
5. Slice leftover ham and turn it into ham and cheese sandwiches, wraps, or quesadillas.
6. Make a cold mixture with chopped ham, sweet pickle relish, chopped celery, enough mayonnaise to moisten the mixture, and salt and pepper. Serve with rolls or lettuce.
7. Prepare fried rice with shredded ham, vegetables, rice, soy sauce, and eggs.

Chickpea Curry

This recipe has an intense flavor that you will love, and in less than twenty minutes, you will be able to enjoy it.

Ingredients

- 1 tbsp curry powder
- Olive oil
- 1-piece peeled ginger
- 2 garlic cloves
- 1 tbsp soft rice

- 1 15-ounce can of chickpeas, rinsed
- 1 small, chopped apple
- 1 tbsp coconut milk
- 1 tbsp chicken broth
- ¼ golden raisins
- Chopped cilantro

Method of preparation

1. Cook the rice according to package directions.
2. Meanwhile, chop the garlic, onion, and ginger in a food processor. Heat 1 tablespoon of oil in a large saucepan over a medium fire. Add the vegetable mixture, stirring frequently, and cook for 5 minutes.
3. Add curry powder, stir and cook for 1 minute. Add chickpeas, apples, coconut milk, chicken broth, raisins, and simmer.
4. Serve over rice and top with cilantro leaves if desired.

Bean and Rice Casserole

This is a casserole that you can prepare with the rice you have in the pantry, and it will be very flavorful.

Ingredients

- 3 tbsp onion, chopped
- 2 garlic cloves, chopped
- 2 tbsp olive oil

- 1-ounce pine nuts
- 1 tbsp butter
- 1 ¼ cup rice
- 2 tsp rosemary, chopped
- 1 tsp salt
- 1 can cream of mushroom soup
- 3 ¼ cups chicken broth
- 1 bag vainitas
- 1 cup cheese whatever you have, grate it; this is optional
- Cooking spray or whatever you have

Method of preparation

1. Preheat the oven to 350°F. Grease an 8×8-inch heatproof baking pan with oil when the oven reaches temperature.
2. In a small skillet, melt the butter over a medium heat, place the pine nuts and sauté, frequently stirring, until the pine nuts are golden brown. Set aside.
3. Heat the oil in a large saucepan over a medium-high fire and add the garlic, onion, rosemary, and 1/2 teaspoon of salt. Fry everything together, stirring constantly, for about one minute. Next, place the rice in the pot and stir-fry for 1–2 minutes, stirring occasionally. Then pour in the broth and bring it to a boil; set the heat to low once it starts to boil. Cover and heat for 28–32 minutes, or until the rice is cooked through and absorbs the liquid. Remove the rice from the heat and test it with a fork.
4. Place the rice, soup, green beans, and salt in a large bowl. Mix the ingredients well and set them aside.

5. Add the rice mixture to a greased baking dish and sprinkle cheese on top. Cover the container loosely with aluminum foil and bake for 15 minutes. After this time, carefully remove the foil and bake for another 15 minutes so that the cheese melts and the green beans are tender. Remove the casserole dish from the oven and sprinkle with pine nuts.
6. Serve this green bean casserole hot.

Traditional Recipe With a Mexican Twist

If you want to try a new dish for your Thanksgiving meal or anytime you want, try this version of traditional green bean casserole with cooked rice, seasoning, green beans, toasted pine nuts, and a touch of Mexican-style cheese such as Manchego, Oaxacan or other varieties such as Cotija.

This delicious baked casserole with cream of mushroom soup and fresh or frozen green beans is the perfect dish to create a new tradition with family or friends. Plus, you can add this recipe to your list of dishes made with typical fall ingredients like vegetables and nuts.

What Is Parboiled Rice?

Parboiled rice is characterized by being partially boiled in the husk before being processed for consumption. The husk helps the rice retain more of its natural vitamins and minerals so that you can get more whole grains in your meals! On top of that, this type of processing gives the rice a subtle nutty flavor, which will make your meal even more delicious!

Vegan Green Hummus

If you don't have meat to eat, but want something with protein, then here it is.

Ingredients

- Paprika
- Salt
- Oil
- 2 garlic cloves
- Juice of a lemon
- 3 spoonful's sesame paste
- 400 g (14 oz) canned chickpeas

Method of preparation

1. Drain the chickpeas, but do not discard the liquid (either from cooking or canning) and pour them into a food processor or blender bowl.
2. Add 1/2 cup of liquid, garlic, tahini, salt, and lemon juice.
3. Process until smooth and creamy.
4. Add more liquid to desired consistency, adjusting the amount of lemon, salt, and garlic to taste.
5. Remember that it should be like a liquid cream, not too thick.
6. Serve on a plate, and drizzle with a bit of olive oil and paprika.

Grilled Venison

I don't think you eat grilled food very often, so you'll like this recipe. Whether you hunt it on your own or have it canned or frozen, here's what you can do.

Ingredients

- Salt
- Black pepper
- Olive oil
- Tomatoes
- 250 ml white wine
- 1 lettuce
- 2 potatoes
- ½ k (1.1 lb.) venison loin

Method of preparation

1. Soak the meat in white wine the day before. Start by seasoning the venison and then take it to the grill. Cook the potatoes with a pinch of salt to obtain rich mashed potatoes.
2. Separately, on a plate, add some lettuce leaves and tomatoes with a pinch of salt and mashed potatoes on the side.
3. Once you have prepared the dish in which we will serve the roasted venison, start preparing the meat. Place the venison directly on the grill or in a baking dish, lightly grease, and season the meat on both sides.
4. Put the meat on the grill for about 2 minutes to brown.

Even if you toughen it too much on the outside, the inside will be tender. Once the meat is done, remove it from the grill and cut it into slices.

5. To finish and serve the roast venison, place the meat on the same plate as the vegetables, season with salt and pepper, and finish with a drizzle of olive oil on top. Your roasted venison is ready to enjoy.
6. Since venison has a very strong flavor, to reduce it, you can marinate it in white wine or milk the day before preparing it.

Chicken Fried Rice

Any fried rice recipe is perfect for a quick meal. Once you have all the ingredients, this recipe is very easy, and since you'll be using a mix of canned chicken and vegetables, dinner can be ready in about 15 minutes.

It would help if you had cold rice to make five ingredients of chicken fried rice if you are craving it on the way home and don't want to stop at a Chinese takeout. Instead of buying a meal high in sodium and MSG, you can just buy takeout rice and prepare a healthy dish in minutes.

All you need to enjoy this simple recipe is a green salad tossed with some mushrooms, drizzled with a simple vinaigrette, or a fruit salad made with seasonal fruits.

Ingredients

- 3 tbsp low sodium soy sauce
- Egg powder
- 1 tbsp peanut oil
- 2 cups diced chicken
- 3 cups cold cooked rice
- 2 cups frozen bell pepper and onion stir-fry mix
- 1 tbsp peanut or safflower oil

Method of preparation

1. Heat a wok or a 10-inch heavy skillet over a medium fire.
2. Add 1 tablespoon of oil and swirl the wok or skillet to coat. Pour the frozen stir-fry mixture into the wok. Cook and stir until crisp-tender, about 2 to 4 minutes. Then add the cold rice and drained opal cubes. Stir-fry these ingredients for 5 minutes until they are all hot.
3. Push the cooked mixture to the sides of the wok or frying pan. Add the extra tablespoon of oil, followed by the egg powder. Heat and whisk the eggs over a medium fire until thickened and cooked through. Stir the mixture with all the other ingredients and add the soy sauce. Stir and serve immediately.

Tuna Casserole in a Clay Pot

Tuna casserole is a classic comforting meal. It's also great for feeding a family in the bunker and taking advantage of what you have in your pantry. You can stock up on discounts at the grocery store or supermarket.

For this recipe, get canned tuna and creamed celery from your pantry and some frozen peas. You need time to cook the noodles before adding them to the slow cooker. This recipe is easy to combine with different contours and offers a variety of alternatives that you can use from your pantry.

Ingredients

- 3 tbsp buttered breadcrumbs
- 10 ounces of medium noodles or pasta
- 2 7-ounce cans of tuna fish, drained
- 1 10-ounce package of peas
- 2 tbsp parsley flakes
- 2/3 cups milk
- 1/3 cup chicken broth
- 2 (10.5 ounce) cans of celery cream

Method of preparation

1. Gather the ingredients.
2. Grease the bottom and sides of the slow cooker with non-stick cooking spray and insert a 4- to 5-quart crockpot.

3. In a large bowl, combine the cream of celery soup, chicken broth, milk, parsley, peas, and tuna.
4. Stir in the cooked noodles or pasta.
5. Pour the mixture into the prepared slow cooker.
6. Coat with chunks of butter. Cover and cook on low for 4 to 6 hours.

There may be variations in the recipe:

- You can use canned chicken, turkey, or salmon in place of tuna; you can also use leftover rotisserie chicken.
- Substitute cream of mushroom soup or chicken broth for the celery cream. Consider adding some chopped celery to the mixture.
- Use potato chip crumbs instead of buttered breadcrumbs.

Chicken Salad Stuffed Avocado Recipe

Preparing a healthy lunch can be a challenge when you're cooped up and often leads to unhealthy fast-food choices.

Make it easier by having chicken ready to go whenever you are. You can prepare a meal in less than 10 minutes with this recipe. You can make it as hot as you want, but the amount you see here makes it moderately spicy without giving you a runny nose. When you buy hot sauce, read the label, some contain sugar, and some brands don't, but if you pay attention to the ingredients list, you can find the right sauce.

If you're not a real avocado fan and dislike the taste a bit, don't worry, the spicy touch is the star of this recipe. The avocado just makes it a creamy filling and allows it to blend with the mayonnaise.

Ingredients

- ¼ tsp salt
- 1 tbsp buffalo sauce
- 1 tbsp lemon juice
- ¼ cup mayonnaise
- 3 cups cooked chicken breast, canned or what's available
- 2 avocados
- Pepper to taste

Method of preparation

1. Start by gathering the ingredients.
2. Place the avocado halves on a plate and scoop out some of the flesh from the center to make ½ a cup of mashed avocado. Set them aside while you prepare the rest of the filling.
3. In a bowl, put the mashed avocado, chicken, mayonnaise, and lime juice; mix well. Then add the buffalo sauce, salt, and pepper. Taste and adjust spices as needed.
4. Spoon this filling evenly into each avocado half. Sprinkle with more buffalo sauce if desired.
5. Enjoy immediately or refrigerate until ready to serve.

CHAPTER 3
SOUPS

Now we are going to prepare soups. These can be eaten for lunch, dinner, or whenever you feel like it. You can enjoy them, and all of them can be made with the ingredients you have in your pantry.

Pinto Bean and Rice Soup

We try beans again, but now using pinto beans, which makes for an enjoyable and tasty meal.

Ingredients

- 1 ½ liters water
- 2 tsp cumin powder
- 1 tbsp chili powder
- 2 red peppers, chopped into squares
- 1 tbsp olive oil
- 5 crushed garlic cloves
- 3 medium onions in squares
- 1-pound pinto beans
- If you have ½ lb. of canned chorizos, you can substitute any other protein
- 2 lbs. tomatoes, chopped
- 2 cups chicken broth
- 2 tbsp tomato paste
- 12 tsp lemon juice
- ½ cup chopped coriander

Method of preparation

1. Rinse the beans, boil them for 2 minutes, then let them soak for 1 hour.
2. Add olive oil to a frying pan and fry the onion and garlic until soft, then add the paprika and cumin.
3. Next, drain the beans, put them in a pot with 1 1/2 liters of water, and cover; cook over a low heat for 1 hour.

4. Once cooked, add the sausage, tomatoes, chicken broth, and tomato sauce, simmer for about 20 minutes, then serve with lime juice and chopped cilantro.

Italian Soup

Italians have a wonderful culinary tradition, and in this section, I will show you how to prepare this recipe quickly and with whatever you have in your bunker.

Ingredients

- 1 ½ cup diced cheese, if you have it
- ½ tsp oregano
- 1 large spoonful of chopped fresh basil
- 1 packet of chicken noodle soup
- 5 cups of hot water
- 1 cup chopped tomato
- ½ a cup chopped celery
- 1 garlic clove
- ½ tbsp olive oil

Method of preparation

1. Heat the oil and sauté the garlic, celery, and tomatoes for three minutes in a pot. Pour the water and add the chicken noodle soup.
2. Cook for 8 minutes and add the basil and oregano. Remove from heat and serve with cheese immediately.

Bean Soup

Beans in soup are very delicious and nutritious. With them, you will have a complete meal and feel full.

Ingredients

- ½ cup whipped cream
- ½ lb chopped bacon
- ½ cup oil
- 1 chopped onion
- 3 liters of water
- 1 lb. red beans

Method of preparation

1. Open the can of beans and remove the damaged beans and impurities. Place them in a container and cover them with water, let them rest overnight. The next day, remove the soaking water and rinse them.
2. Cook them in a pot full of water. When it starts to boil, add ½ cup of cold water, repeat 3 times, and add the onion and oil. Add the bacon and simmer for about two hours when it starts to boil again.
3. After two hours, season with salt, add a little whipped cream, and serve.

White Bean Soup

Now I want to show you how to make a white bean soup that you will love.

Ingredients

- ½ green chili
- 1 onion
- A bunch of cilantro
- 6 garlic cloves
- 1 lb. canned or preserved smoked ribs
- 1 lb. white beans
- Water
- A dash of red sauce
- 1 can of tomato paste
- 3 cubes of chicken flavor bouillon

Method of preparation

1. Boil the beans in hot water. Sauté the ribs in a skillet. When the beans are tender (not too tender), add the ribs about an hour after cooking starts.
2. Take a cup of beans, mix with celery, garlic, onion, and cilantro, and add them to the soup. To finish flavoring, add the chicken bouillon cubes.

Bean Noodle Soup With Pasta

This noodle soup is the perfect idea for a light stew. It is a black bean soup, made with a squeeze of lemon and pasta to make a full and nutritious dish, but with fewer calories than usual.

It is ideal for spring or early spring when the cold has not quite passed, but the body starts to demand lighter dishes. Keep reading and learn how to prepare a delicious bean soup with pasta and a touch of lemon that you will love!

Ingredients

- 1 onion
- 1 celery
- 2 carrots
- 3 leek leaves
- 3 cloves of garlic
- 2 pieces of lemon zest
- 100 g (3.52 oz) canned black bean
- 3 tablespoons tomato sauce
- 1 teaspoon sweet paprika
- ½ teaspoon cumin
- ½ teaspoon ginger
- 1 teaspoon dried thyme
- 1½ liter water
- 1 pinch of salt and pepper
- 50 g (1.76 oz) thin noodles

Method of preparation

1. To start preparing this delicious black bean soup, the first thing to do is have the ingredients ready. To do this, wash, peel and cut all the vegetables into small pieces.
2. Cut the leeks into thick pieces, the rest into smaller pieces, or to your taste. Remember that the lemon zest should be two wide strips, which you can get by passing a potato peeler lengthwise.
3. Once all the ingredients are ready, put them all together with the seasoning and water. Leave the salt and pepper for last. Reserve the beans and pasta separately.
4. Heat the pressure cooker until it beeps and continue cooking for 10 minutes. After this time, remove the cooker from the heat, check that the vegetables are tender, and mix everything with the help of a hand blender. Correct the seasoning if necessary.
5. Once everything is blended, return the pot to the heat and add the beans and noodles. Cook until the pasta is ready. Note that the soup may become thicker or thinner; you can always add more water or vegetable broth to change the consistency.
6. Serve the bean soup with the pasta and garnish with a bit of oil and a pinch of fresh thyme. Remember, the secret of this noodle soup is the lemon zest, so be sure to add it.

White Rice Soup

This is a delicious and very nutritious soup that you will love.

Ingredients

- 1-pound broth
- A pinch of salt
- 100 g rice
- A little egg powder
- 50 g ham

Method of preparation

1. Place the broth in a saucepan. Heat over medium fire and use a spoon to remove the fat that has formed on the surface.
2. Cook the egg powder in a pot with water. Chop the ham.
3. When the broth is boiling, add the rice and cook for 20 minutes. Set it aside.
4. Add the eggs and ham and serve immediately.

Noodle Soup

We all love noodle soup. This one is very good, and you will love its flavor, plus it will leave everyone satisfied.

Ingredients

- 1 medium onion
- 1-liter water
- 3 garlic cloves
- 3 tablespoons oil
- 1 teaspoon salt
- 3 bay leaves
- 3 tablespoons mayonnaise
- 2 tablespoons butter
- 1 small package of noodles
- 1 cup of cream
- 3 tablespoons mayonnaise
- 1 tablespoon granulated chicken broth
- ½ cup grated cheese

Method of preparation

1. Fill a large pot with water and add salt. Add the onion, garlic, bay leaf, and oil. Heat over a high fire until it starts to boil, then add the pasta. Heat uncovered until the pasta is cooked "al dente," about 12 minutes.
2. Heat the butter in a skillet over a medium fire and add the pasta.
3. Combine with the mayonnaise, cream, broth, and cheese. Stir until completely coated. Cook for 3 minutes before serving.

Taco Soup

Tacos are not only eaten Mexican style. You can also make a soup with the ingredients; here I will show you how to do it.

Ingredients

- ½ k (1.1 lb.) canned or preserved ground beef
- 1 tbsp cornstarch or two tbsp corn flour
- 14 oz chicken broth
- 1 can green enchilada sauce
- 1 can of sweet corn
- 1 can of chopped tomatoes
- 1 can of black beans, drained or rinsed

Method of preparation

1. Add all the beans, tomatoes, corn, hot sauce, and chicken broth to a large pot. Stir to combine. Cover and cook on low heat for 3 hours.
2. Mix cornmeal or cornstarch with water to make a paste. Add to the soup and stir. This will help thicken the soup.
3. Add ground beef to the pot and stir to combine.
4. Serve warm with grated cheese and tortilla strips.

Tex-Mex Soup

Following the same style as the previous recipe, this soup is also very tasty and comes with that Mexican touch that you will surely love.

Ingredients

- Oregano to taste
- Salt and pepper to taste
- 2½ cups chicken broth
- ½ cup salsa taquera
- ½ cup tomato puree
- 1 diced tomato
- 1½ cups drained beans
- ½ green bell pepper in cubes
- 1 cup drained corn
- If you don't have chorizo, you can substitute it for the protein of your choice.

For the garnish, you need:

- Chopped cilantro
- Cheese if you have it, grated
- Tortilla chips
- A cup of cream

Method of preparation

1. Fry the chopped chorizo in its fat. Remove the excess oil, and add the corn, the bell pepper, and the beans; add the tomato last so it doesn't fall apart.
2. Pour the tomato puree and let it cook a little to reduce the acidity.
3. Add the salsa taquera, pour in the chicken broth, and mix well.
4. Season with salt, pepper, and oregano.
5. Serve with fried corn, yellow cheese, cream, and a pinch of chopped cilantro.

Peanut Butter Soup

Peanut butter soup is an oriental dish with a bold and very healthy taste. Peanuts and curry will give character to a soup that stands out for its creaminess. Some of these vegetables are an ideal backdrop for strong flavors that are highly recommended for the cold autumn. A simple preparation based on peanut butter and cream will turn any soup into a joyful ritual, spoon after spoon. We will discover a tradition that will transport us miles away. Prepare this exotic and comforting peanut butter soup that you will love.

Ingredients

- 4 egg yolks
- 750 ml vegetable broth
- 150 g (5.29 oz) peanut butter
- 250 ml cream to cook
- 1 tbsp curry
- Salt and pepper to taste

Method of preparation

1. Take the liquid ingredients and put them in a saucepan to boil. Also, add the peanut butter and curry. Add salt and pepper to taste.
2. Beat the yolks with the cream. This way you will have a creamy and smooth result.
3. When you have the mixture ready, gradually place the eggs with the cream in the broth. Go easy heating just enough to make it look creamy.
4. It may take about 10 minutes to thicken completely; do not stop stirring. Use a wooden spoon for the best results.
5. When it's ready, turn off the heat and let it rest.

Black Bean Soup

This black bean soup is also delicious and packed with protein.

Ingredients

- ¼ cup lime juice
- ⅓ cup olive oil
- 2½ cups of water
- 4 cans of black beans, drained
- 2 tablespoons seasoning
- 1 tablespoon Maggi dehydrated soup
- Lime slices
- 1 chopped red onion

Method of preparation

1. Sauté the onion in a large pot over medium heat for 3 minutes or until slightly translucent and fragrant. Remove from heat.
2. Place the remaining soup ingredients: beans, water, oil, lime juice, and broth in a blender and blend until very smooth.
3. Return this mixture to the same pot and cook over a medium heat, occasionally stirring, until heated through and thickened. Season with salt if desired.
4. Serve with half of the cream and onion and add a few slices of lime.

Kale Soup

A nutritious healthy soup.

Ingredients

- Olive oil
- 20 g (0.7 oz) of parsley
- Salt
- Pepper
- 2 cloves of garlic
- 70 g (0.7 oz) celery
- 50 g (1.76 oz) carrots
- 100 g (3.52 oz) onions
- 140 g (4.93 oz) bread
- 340 g (11.9 oz) kale

Method of preparation

1. Cut the bread into slices not too thick and put it in the toaster. Now prepare the vegetables, and cut the onion, carrot, and celery into small pieces. Chop the garlic and kale into small pieces.
2. Heat a little oil in a frying pan over a medium fire and sauté the onion and garlic. In a saucepan, heat water and add it along with the carrots and celery. Stir well. Let it cook for a few minutes.
3. Now add the kale to the broth and stir. Season with salt and pepper. Cover and let it simmer until the soup thickens for about 15 minutes. Serve in a bowl and finish with parsley leaves and enjoy!

CHAPTER 4
DINNERS

It's time to make delicious dinners. Eating three meals a day is even more important during difficult times to ensure that you and your family remain healthy, as access to medical help may be limited.

Beef Stew

This is a delicious stew, not heavy, and very complete at a nutritional level, and the best thing is that you can make it with whatever you have in the pantry.

Ingredients

- 1 small potato peeled and cut into cubes
- 2 tbsp olive oil
- ½ cup sweet corn
- 2 tbsp sofrito
- 2 garlic cloves
- 1 can tomato sauce
- 1 tsp oregano dried
- ½ cup of water
- 1 bay leaf
- 1 can of corned beef
- Salt and ground black pepper

Method of preparation

1. Bring a small pot of water to a boil. Add the potatoes and cook uncovered until slightly tender, for about 5 minutes. Drain with a slotted spoon.
2. Heat the oil in a large skillet or pot over a medium-high fire. Add drained potatoes, corn, sofrito, and garlic; cook and stir until fragrant, for about 2 to 3 minutes. Add tomato paste, oregano, and bay leaves; cook and stir until flavors are combined, for about 2 to 3 minutes. Add water and

bring the mixture to a boil. Reduce heat to medium-low and add the corned beef. Cook until heated through, for about 6 to 8 minutes.

White Beans in Green Sauce

This is the way to prepare these beans:

Ingredients

- 1 bell pepper or ½ tsp bell pepper pulp
- 200 ml vegetable broth
- 75 ml white wine
- 4 tbsp parsley chopped
- 2 garlic cloves
- Olive oil
- 400 g (14.1 oz) white beans, cooked and drained
- Salt

Method of preparation

1. Coat the bottom of the pan with a thin layer of olive oil.
2. Heat over medium fire and add the chopped garlic. Let it brown a little and add chopped parsley.
3. Cut open the peppers and put them in the pot with the pulp inside, rubbing the bottom with a wooden spoon. Add a pinch of bell pepper flesh and stir.
4. Pour in the white wine and cook for a few minutes.
5. Put the beans into the pot, spread them out without break-

ing them, and add the broth.
6. Keep the heat on low for about 10 minutes while gently shaking the pot to combine the sauce.
7. Be sure to taste it for salt and serve immediately.

Pressure Canned Venison

Venison is very delicious, and here's how to make it even tastier.

Ingredients

- Black pepper to taste
- ½ cup milk
- Olive oil to taste
- 800 ml cooking cream
- ½ tsp curry powder
- 1 carrot
- 1 onion
- 500 g (17.63 oz) venison meat or any meat you have
- Salt to taste

Method of preparation

1. Cut all the meat into small pieces (squares).
2. Put the meat in a container with milk for two days before serving. I recommend you put a pinch of curry in the container with the milk so that the meat acquires its flavor.
3. In a saucepan, sauté a julienned onion and a chopped car-

rot. When the vegetables are browned, put all the pieces of meat in the pan, add a little curry powder and a pinch of black pepper if desired; stir-fry until the pieces of meat are browned.
4. When the meat looks brown, fill the pot with water to cover all the meat. Add a little olive oil.
5. Cook until the meat is tender. This may take about 3 or 4 hours. As the meat is quite tough, it is recommended to cook it first on high heat and then lower it little by little. When cooking, fill the pot with water, and never leave the meat exposed. You can add a little curry powder to add extra flavor.
6. When the meat is tender (easy to break with a fork), reduce the water to the measure of only two fingers, then add the contents of 800 ml of cooking cream. Pour in the curry powder and mix well with the cream. Add more curry if you desire a spicier flavor. Add a dash of black pepper.
7. Let the sauce thicken, stir well and let it reduce, according to whether you prefer more or less sauce; it is ready to serve. This dish goes perfectly with a little white rice and, if possible, basmati accompanies it the best.

Venison Medallions

Venison medallions are something you've probably never tasted. Here's how to prepare this delicious meal.

Ingredients

- 1½ lb. venison tenderloin
- 12 prunes, remove the pits
- 1 sprig of fresh rosemary
- 350 ml beef broth
- 1/4 tsp salt
- Freshly ground pepper
- 1/4 tsp ground cinnamon
- ¼ tsp ground cloves
- 135 ml red wine
- 50 g (1.76 oz) butter
- 1 chopped onion
- 1 garlic clove, minced

Method of preparation

1. Combine the red wine, plums, thyme, and broth and boil for 3 minutes.
2. Remove, cover, and set aside.
3. Cut the venison into slices.
4. Mix salt, pepper, cinnamon, and cloves, and sprinkle over the meat.
5. Melt the butter over medium-high heat, then fry the medallions for 4 minutes on each side.

6. Remove them from the saucepan and keep them warm.
7. In the same saucepan, sauté the onion and garlic without letting them brown, then add the wine mixture.
8. Bring to a boil, reduce heat and reduce liquid by half.
9. Adjust seasonings.
10. Drizzle with the sauce after serving.

Roasted Deer

This is the venison you will surely love to have in your bunker. I'm going to show you how to make it.

Ingredients

- 250 g (8.8 oz) raw and sliced ham
- 250 g (8.8 oz) butter
- 1 cup heavy cream.
- 1 venison piece, if you hunt it and have a leg, much better.
- Salt
- Ground pepper.

Method of preparation

1. Clean the legs by removing the skin. Make some cuts with a sharp knife.
2. Mix it with the slices of ham, and season with salt and pepper.
3. Brush the legs thoroughly with butter and sprinkle with salt and pepper again.

4. Butter a baking dish and place the legs in it. Then, put it in the oven, which should have a temperature of 250°F (120°C), and let it cook for a few minutes.
5. Take it out and grease it again with butter.
6. Put it into the oven again. Repeat this several times, basting with butter and adding a little hot water to the meat.
7. When the legs are fully cooked and browned on all sides, serve immediately, topped with cream.

Dried Meat

This is a very spicy version. If you don't like spicy food, I suggest you modify the recipe. To obtain a sweet version, you can try marinating the meat with honey, brown sugar, and pineapple juice.

Ingredients

- A beer that you have in the bunker
- 2 tbsp sauce
- 500 g beef or pork
- 1 tbsp thyme
- Pepper to taste
- Paprika to taste
- A pinch of cumin
- chili powder to taste

Method of preparation

1. Clean and remove the fat from the meat.
2. Cut into thin strips, 1/4" thick and 1" wide (measurements do not have to be exact).
3. To prepare the marinade, add the sauce, beer, a pinch of salt, and a little honey.
4. I recommend you previously prepare the marinade to make things easier.
5. Put the meat into the refrigerator for 12 hours.
6. Once the meat is marinated, remove it from the refrigerator, dry it with a paper towel and add the dry ingredients, which are: pepper, cumin, thyme, and paprika. Cover the meat well with this mixture.
7. Put the meat on the baking sheet and cook at 140-160ºF (~65ºC) for 4 hours, leaving the oven door ajar to allow the moisture to escape.
8. Check the meat occasionally and turn the strips over to dry as well.
9. Once the meat is dry and tough, rough and silky looking, it is ready. It can be stored in a bag or jar with a hole in the lid (so moisture can escape).

Hardtack

Hardtack is tough because it does not contain yeast, which lasts a long time. Yeast is a type of bacteria that helps bread rise, making it light and soft but also brittle and fragile.

Skipping the yeast (and any other perishable ingredients) will make your bread last longer and make it the perfect meal for a long journey.

The method of preparation is very simple; only three ingredients are needed:

Ingredients

- 2 cups of flour
- 1½ cup of water
- 2 tsp salt

For every two cups of flour, use one cup of water plus one cup of salt.

Method of preparation

1. Mix these ingredients until you obtain a consistent, smooth, and non-sticky dough (add more flour if it is necessary). Next, roll out the dough, cut it into squares and pierce with a fork.
2. Bake it in the oven at about 370ºF (~190ºC) until they are

very firm. Put it in a pan, add a little flour and cook over medium heat for an hour until firm.
3. After the cookies are cooked, let them cool to firm up more; then store them in a cool, dry place. They last a long time. One of my cookies has been in the paper bag for over 3 months, and they are still intact.

Fun fact: this is seen in many movies. In The Lord of the Rings series, Frodo and Sam carry it on their journey to Mordor.

Cereal Bars

These bars can also be stored almost forever. If you wonder what the expiration date is, they'll tell you it's what it says on the box, but in reality, they last forever—all the other ingredients separately should last about 20 years! Of course, you must maintain them properly. Some time ago, I put two bars in a plastic bag, and they look perfect, even after 6 months.

Ingredients

- 3 tbsp honey
- 3 tbsp water
- 1 package Jell-O
- 1 cup brown sugar or what you have
- 2 ½ cups powdered milk
- 2 cups oatmeal

Method of preparation

1. Combine the oatmeal, powdered milk, and sugar in a large bowl.
2. In a medium saucepan, combine the jell, water, and honey, then boil the mixture over a medium-low heat for about 3 minutes. Remember: you will only use 3 tablespoons of water, not the amount indicated on the jell package.
3. Once the jell is boiled, mix with a spoon or a hand mixer if you don't have electricity; it may be difficult to mix at first. You can add a little water, but only a small amount.
4. Once the mixture is smooth and consistent, transfer it to a square baking sheet lined with wax paper and bake at 200ºF (~95ºC) for 1 hour. If you have a dehydrator, you can use it, but I prefer toasted bars.

Stir-Fried Vegetables

No matter the conditions in which you find yourself, no decent home can be without this recipe. There are many recipes, but this one is so simple that you can make it with whatever you have in the bunker, and you will enjoy it.

Ingredients

- 2 zucchinis
- 1 Italian green bell pepper
- 2 Italian red peppers

- 3 onions
- Olive oil
- Salt to taste

Method of preparation

1. Coat the bottom of a large frying pan with oil. Heat over a medium fire and add the chopped onion. Sauté over medium-low heat until soft and almost translucent, no more than 10 minutes.
2. Then add the chopped peppers and continue to fry until the peppers change color.
3. Add the diced zucchini and continue frying until the zucchini changes color and softens.
4. If you wish, you can add some fried tomatoes to this mix.
5. Pack in jars or put them in Ziplock freezer bags and freeze in portions as needed, only if you have electricity or a refrigerator.

Uses: you can add to any cooked vegetables and use them as a bed for grilled meats or grilled fish. It can also be served on toast topped with canned tuna, smoked meats, or anything you can think of for any quick dinner or lunch.

Homemade Fried Tomato

Ingredients

- 2 kgs (4.4 lbs.) tomatoes
- 2 tbsp sugar
- 1 tsp salt
- 4 tbsp olive oil
- 2 cups of water

Method of preparation

1. Put a liter of water to boil, cut the tomatoes from the bottom and pass them for 20 seconds through the boiling water. Then put them into cold water to refresh them.
2. Scald the tomatoes
3. Peel the skin of the tomatoes.
4. Chop and grind them in the blender.
5. Put the olive oil in the pan and when it is hot, remove from the heat, add the tomato, the salt, and half the sugar. Attach a lid that has vent holes for steam. Put it on a medium heat for 10 minutes and stir with a wooden spoon preferably.
6. After 25 minutes you can remove the lid, add the rest of the sugar, and in about 50 minutes you will have the recipe ready.
7. Taste and confirm if it lacks salt or sugar and then enjoy.

Chicken Soup

Ingredients

- 3 or 4 chicken carcasses, breast or a couple of thighs. According to your taste
- 2 liters of water
- Chopped vegetables to taste
- Bay leaves to taste
- 1 cup of rice or pasta
- 2 garlic cloves minced

Method of preparation

1. Boil the chicken carcasses or the pieces you have chosen with the water.
2. Add the chopped vegetables, garlic, and bay leaf; let it boil.
3. You won't have the broth Grandma used to make, but at least you'll have something to enjoy.

Indian Stir-Fry

It takes a little while to prepare the produce but if it is plentiful and in season, you will love it. You can add chunks of canned fish, olives, and more. Of course, drain well because vegetables swimming in the wash water are neither pretty nor fresh.

Ingredients

- 1-piece fresh ginger
- 3 garlic cloves
- Olive oil to taste
- 1 stick celery
- 2 eggplants
- 2 red peppers
- 3 onions
- 1 ½ tbsp ground cumin
- 1 tsp ground cinnamon
- ½ tsp cardamom seeds
- 1 ½ tbsp coriander seeds
- 1 tsp ground cayenne
- 1200 g (2.64 lbs.) crushed tomato (the one that you have in conserve)
- Salt to taste

Method of preparation

1. Coat the bottom of a large skillet or frying pan with oil, and heat over a medium fire.
2. Sauté the chopped or sliced onion until tender, then add

the chopped peppers and celery sticks. Continue frying until they change color.
3. Add the diced eggplant and sauté until softened, stirring occasionally.
4. Meanwhile, prepare the spices and seasonings. Crush the garlic, and grind or grate the peeled ginger to a puree.
5. Grind coriander seeds and cardamom. Combine with cinnamon, chili, and cumin.
6. Add all the seasonings and fry a little to enhance their flavor when the vegetables are ready.
7. Add the crushed tomatoes, stir to combine, and continue frying over a low heat until the tomato water is consumed, resulting in a thick, spicy green tomato sauce.

Uses for the basic curry or Indian stir-fry, include:

- As a vegetarian stew or on its own.
- Add chopped meats, cooked vegetables, rice, or pasta.
- Add other vegetables that just need cooking, like spinach.

It will keep well in the refrigerator for several days, or you can eat it all right away.

Spicy Fried Chickpeas

Not only are they served with fresh vegetables in the form of salads in the summer, but they can also enrich any vegetable stew or can be added to the stir-fries previously mentioned. These are one of the quality vegetable preserves that will make your life easier. One advantage of preparing this spicy fried chickpea recipe is that it works very well as a first course or as a healthy appetizer, and it is ready in a jiffy.

Ingredients

- 1 tbsp turmeric
- 3-4 tbsp olive oil
- Salt to taste
- 1 tbsp garlic salt
- 200 g (7 oz) canned chickpeas

Method of preparation

1. Drain the chickpeas from the liquid.
2. Put a little oil (3-4 tablespoons) into a frying pan and heat over a high fire.
3. Add and sauté the chickpeas until the water evaporates, stirring occasionally.
4. Add the spices and a little salt. Stir well and continue frying until toasted on the outside.

CHAPTER 5
SNACKS

As I mentioned before, you shouldn't miss out on the foods you love to eat by being cooped up during a catastrophe. The plan for us preppers is to be ready for whatever happens, and snacks are a must. So, I'm going to share with you a series of delicious recipes that you can make with whatever you have in the bunker.

Rhubarb Cream

With this cream, you can combine many foods creating a delicious flavor.

Ingredients

- 150 g (5.29 oz) sugar
- ½ kg (1.1 lb.) rhubarb

Method of preparation

1. Put the rhubarb in a pot.
2. Pour the sugar and shake or stir lightly.
3. This allows the sugar to take effect at room temperature, and after about 30 minutes, you will see the rhubarb juice begin to accumulate at the bottom of the pot.
4. When it starts to boil, cover and simmer.
5. Cook for about 20 minutes and check the texture by stirring the contents of the pot; you should not see large chunks but a uniform cream.
6. When your rhubarb cream is ready, let it cool and then store it in the refrigerator in an airtight container.
7. Taste the cream when it cools to see if you need to add a little more sugar.

Energy Bars

Energy bars can be a delicious and practical snack to take with you and eat when you are away from home because they will leave you feeling full.

Ingredients

- 500 g (1.1 lb.) oatmeal
- Dehydrated fruit to taste, according to the flavor you wish to achieve.
- A handful of almonds
- 1 tsp cinnamon
- 2 tbsp honey
- A drizzle of olive oil

Method of preparation

It's simple, and you don't need to do too much to prepare them. There are molds to prepare, but if you don't have any, I want to see what you can do with the lid of a cardboard box, such as a shoebox. This is how I have made them, and you can see that they look very delicious. Line the box's lid with parchment or baking paper, and that's it. I recommend this type of paper. Otherwise, they will stick, and you won't be able to remove them.

Now, assemble your DIY molds. You can make them however you like. Let's start with the recipe, and you will see in no time that you will have homemade energy bars without an oven, perfect for your breakfast, lunch, or dinner.

1. First, weigh your ingredients. Add hazelnuts and almonds or your favorite nuts. Chop them with a knife to be about the same size, but do not grind them in a blender or food processor.
2. Chop the dehydrated fruit a little too.
3. In a wide frying pan, about 20 cm (8 in) in diameter, put a tablespoon of oil and add the chopped nuts. Cook over a medium heat. Stir for a few minutes, then add the oats. Stir and toast slowly for a few more minutes. Now add the cinnamon and dehydrated fruit. Stir for a few more minutes to bring everything together well.
4. Now it is time to add the honey. To make it easier for you, add four tablespoons first, stir and then add another four tablespoons for easier integration. You will gradually see a caramel-like mixture. When your honey has blended with the mixture, it is time to put it into the mold.
5. Pour the mixture into the mold, and with the help of a spatula and a piece of parchment paper to avoid sticking, press the mixture lightly so that it is compact and adapts to the shape of the mold.
6. Cover with parchment paper and refrigerate for at least two hours. When that time has passed, you must remove the "blocks" from the board to cut your twelve bars or as many as you want depending on what size to make them.

Chia Berry Smoothie Bowl

Make smoothie bowls with your favorite flavors. Choose fresh (or dried) fruits like strawberries, bananas, peaches, apples, and others. But you can also use leafy greens like spinach, kale, and celery... even add protein and healthy fats like nuts, coconut oil, flaxseed, or avocado.

Ingredients

- Oat milk
- 1 banana
- 1 kiwi
- 100 g (3.52 oz) strawberries
- 30 g (1 oz) walnuts
- Honey
- 1 tsp chia seeds

Method of preparation

1. Blend all the ingredients, serve and enjoy.

You can also make a refreshing and cleansing version with these ingredients:

- 1 cup of green leaves
- 1 cup of cold green tea
- 1 orange juice
- ½ mango
- ½ cup peach

- 2 mint leaves
- 1 tbsp flax seeds

The process is the same, blend and enjoy.

Strawberry Sorbet

Strawberries are the main ingredient of many desserts we eat every day, and almost everyone eats them as they are so delicious. In addition, the fruit can be used to make smoothies, milkshakes, and ice creams, which are ideal for cooling off in summer.

Ingredients

- ½ lemon juice
- ½ L water
- 250 g (8.8 oz) white sugar
- ½ kg (1.1 lb.) strawberries

Method of preparation

1. First, have your strawberries ready for the sorbet. Wash them, remove the tails, and put them into a saucepan with a little water. Put it on the heat and let the strawberries boil for about 5 minutes.
2. Then, remove the strawberries from the pan, place them on an absorbent paper towel to remove excess moisture, and add them to a blender. Blend the strawberries to a puree texture, and when they are ready, pass them through a strainer to remove the seeds.

3. Now make a syrup for the strawberry sorbet. Put ½ liter of water in a saucepan with sugar over a medium heat to dissolve the sugar. Stir the mixture constantly and add the lemon juice.
4. After about 10 minutes, add the strawberry puree to the syrup and mix all the ingredients. After mixing well, put it into a bowl and take it into the refrigerator. You should take it out every hour to break the ice crystals that have formed and repeat this step until serving time.
5. Follow these steps, and your strawberry sorbet will be ready. You can add a few slices of strawberries for topping and garnish with some mint leaves on the top.

CHAPTER 6
DESSERTS

Like snacks, there is nothing better than enjoying a dessert after a meal. You will find the following recipes not only tasty but easy to make and use quick ingredients.

Green Pudding

This is a very simple and quick pudding to make.

Ingredients

- 3 green onions
- Egg powder
- 2 eggplants
- 1 cup broccoli florets
- 1 tbsp dried herbs
- Salt and pepper
- 4 tbsp olive oil
- 1 cup of peas
- 3 tbsp cream cheese or whatever you need
- If you have it, fontina cheese

Method of preparation

1. Mash the eggplants and fry them in olive oil in a frying pan. Add the peas and cooked broccoli, and season to taste.
2. Put all the vegetables in a blender together with the chopped onion and blend until creamy.
3. Mix the fontina cheese, cream cheese, and egg powder.
4. Prepare this in a buttered and floured pan, cover with aluminum foil and bake in a bain-marie in the oven over a medium heat until you notice that it is firm. Remove, let it rest for 10 minutes, and unmold.

Lentil Candy Bars

These are sweet lentil bars that will help you enjoy great natural proteins.

Ingredients

- 35 g (1.2 oz) sunflower seeds
- 35 g (1.2 oz) almonds
- 35 g (1.2 oz) walnuts
- 35 g (1.2 oz) oat flakes
- 100 g (3.52 oz) cooked lentils
- 50 ml honey
- A pinch of salt

Method of preparation

1. Drain the lentils. Put them fully stretched on a tray lined with baking paper and dry in the oven at 150ºC (302F) for 15 minutes.
2. Once the lentils are dry, remove them from the oven and put all the ingredients in a bowl.
3. Add the warm honey and salt, mix and return to the oven, and bake at 180º (356F) for 20 minutes, stirring occasionally.
4. Let it cool and store in an airtight jar.

Lentils and Dates Brownies

A delicious well-made brownie is very quick to make and exceedingly good.

Ingredients

- 1 tbsp baking powder
- 170 g (5.99 oz) flour
- A drizzle of vanilla extract
- 150 g (5.29 oz) sugar
- 200 g (7 oz) cooked lentils
- 85 cc olive oil
- A pinch of salt
- ½ cup tofu
- 4 tbsp bitter cocoa powder
- ½ cup chocolate chunks

Method of preparation

1. Put into a blender the lentils, tofu, oil, vanilla, and sugar until a dough with a liquid texture is formed.
2. In a bowl, put the flour, cocoa powder, a pinch of salt, and baking powder, and mix these ingredients.
3. Combine the two mixtures with a spatula. It is a dense substance difficult to blend, but with devotion and patience, it can be done. Add the chocolate chips.
4. Preheat the oven for at least 15 minutes. Pre-grease the molds, spatula the mixture into the molds, and bake at a low-medium temperature (170°C-338F) for 60 minutes.

Homemade Ice Cream

You can have it ready in the freezer for whenever you wish to have it. If you have a sweet tooth, you cannot miss this recipe for ice cream wraps.

Ingredients

- 1 cup frozen strawberries
- 1 cup frozen bananas

Method of preparation

1. Process everything in a blender until it obtains the desired texture.
2. Plant-based comfort food is the way forward.

Tangerine Pudding

Tangerine puddings are delicious, made with what you have in the bunker, it will sweeten the confinement.

Ingredients

- 1 cup sugar
- 2 large tangerines
- 1 ½ cups leavening flour
- 100 cc sunflower oil
- Egg powder
- Powdered sugar

For the glaze, you need:

- 20 cc lemon juice
- 250 g (8.8 oz) sugar

Method of preparation

1. Cut one tangerine in half and squeeze, reserving the juice.
2. Now cut the other tangerine in half, seed and slice, and put them into a blender (with skin).
3. Add the oil, egg powder, sugar, and squeezed tangerine juice.
4. Process everything until the peel disappears.
5. Pour the mixture into a bowl and add the flour with circular movements.
6. Grease and flour a pudding mold, put the mixture into the mold, and bake in the oven at 180º (356F) for 45 minutes.
7. Mix the powdered sugar with the lemon juice and pour it over the hot pudding.

CHAPTER 7
FRUITS AND VEGETABLES

With fruits and vegetables, you will be able to prepare a series of recipes. If you have a garden, you will be able to enjoy these delicious recipes. I will show you how to prepare them.

Marinated Grilled Tofu

You also want to know how to cook tofu to make it rich and delicious, right? You are not alone; that is why I have decided to explain how to make marinated grilled tofu here.

Follow these simple tips on how to marinate and bake tofu, and you'll never have bland tofu again.

Even if you're not a vegetarian, or if you are curious to try new things and different flavors, give tofu a try. It is a portion of very healthy food and an excellent choice for adding a plant-based protein source to your dishes.

As a tip, before you start adding it to your recipes, you should learn how to prepare it correctly.

Otherwise, you may end up with tasteless tofu, and you may not be thrilled with the results. It would be a shame if you eliminated this food from your diet just because you did not prepare it appropriately and did not know how to make the most of it.

It is not necessary to marinate tofu. You can even eat it raw if you want since the tofu you bought at the supermarket is already cooked.

However, if you start with this food, you will have to get used to it, and I do not recommend starting with raw tofu. Besides, marinated tofu is much better.

You will marinate it with a mixture of spices, extra virgin olive oil, and soy sauce. This way, the tofu absorbs the flavors of all these ingredients.

Then you must cook the marinated tofu on the grill, as I'll show you in this case. However, you can also bake it in the oven.

Here is the recipe step by step, so you do not miss any detail:

Ingredients

- 2 tbsp soy sauce
- 2 tbsp olive oil
- 4 tbsp sweet paprika
- 4 tbsp dried parsley
- 2 tbsp garlic powder
- 250 g (8.8 oz) firm tofu

Method of preparation

1. Wrap the tofu cubes in a kitchen towel to absorb the water. For best results, it is better to leave it like this for a while, even with some weight on top, to allow it to exert pressure. If not, you can press with your hand to release the water.
2. Cut the tofu into strips or cubes, according to your preference. Put it in a bowl.
3. Add garlic powder, dried parsley, sweet paprika, extra virgin olive oil, and soy sauce. As soy sauce is salty, it is not necessary to add extra salt.

4. Mix everything and try to soak all the tofu. For the tofu to acquire its flavor, the mixture should be allowed to stand. The longer you let it sit, the better. I recommend keeping it in the refrigerator overnight. If that is not possible, then leave it for 1 hour.
5. To cook it, simply pop it in a frying pan. There is no need to add oil; it will be enough to use macerated juice so that it does not stick. Stir it carefully so that it does not break until you see that it acquires a golden and appetizing tone. Serve it immediately.

Avocado Green Salad

Satisfy your appetite with this delicious, easy, and different green salad. Without a doubt, the avocado gives it a special touch; I'll explain it as follows.

Ingredients

For the dressing you need:

- 1 natural yogurt
- ½ cup cilantro
- 2 lemons juice

For the green salad:

- 1 cucumber
- 2 onions

- 1 cup green grapes (remove the stone)
- 4 cups of baby spinach leaves
- ½ cup green pepitas
- 1 avocado chopped into slices
- Salt and pepper to taste

Method of preparation

To make the dressing:

1. Start by blending the ingredients and add salt and pepper. Set aside.

To make the green salad:

1. Remove some of the cucumber peel and scoop out the seeds.
2. Cut it into a half moon shape.
3. Thinly slice the onion and cut the grapes in half.
4. Put in a bowl, spinach leaves, cucumber, onion, and grapes.
5. Pour half of the dressing and seeds in and mix them, taking care not to spoil the ingredients.
6. Serve and arrange the avocado, add more dressing, and sprinkle the remaining seeds on top.

Avocado Hummus

Earlier, we made hummus. Now I want to show you another hummus recipe that you will surely love.

Ingredients

- Lemon juice
- Salt to taste
- 3 garlic cloves
- 3 tbsp sesame oil
- 2 avocados
- 1 cup cooked chickpeas

Method of preparation

1. You can cook the chickpeas yourself, although, in my experience, you get better results using a pot of cooked chickpeas. Drain them and put them into the blender.
2. Scoop the fruit out of the avocado and pour it into a blender with the lemon, oil, whole (but peeled) garlic, and salt.
3. Blend at maximum power until you get a uniformed fine paste. The final color will be chartreuse from the chickpea and avocado mixture. I recommend refrigerating it before serving for a better seal, of course, if you have electricity.

Follow these tips:

- With toasted whole wheat bread or even whole wheat pasta, it tastes better.

- The water from the can of cooked chickpeas can be used to cook other chickpeas with a stronger flavor.
- Avocados are best ripe but not overripe. This way, the hummus will not be overwhelming and will be smoother.

Canned Cranberries

Take advantage of canned cranberries that you can enjoy in many ways.

Ingredients

- 1 cup whipping cream
- 1 package of cream cheese
- 1 cup plain yogurt
- Pinch of salt
- ½ cup of brown sugar
- 1 cup of blueberries
- 1 cup whipping cream
- You can use any nuts you have or seeds

Method of preparation

1. Put the sugar and blueberries in a small saucepan. Cook until the sugar dissolves; then add about 5 more minutes. Remove from heat and pass through a blender.
2. When it is ready, combine cream cheese, yogurt, and whipping cream in another bowl.
3. Slowly stir in the blueberry mixture.

4. Serve in small cups and top with fresh blueberries and some other garnishes like chopped nuts or almonds—even some seeds of your liking.

Sautéed Green Vegetables

Earlier, we made a different version. Now, I will show you how to make one with green vegetables.

Ingredients

- 1 tbsp honey
- 1 cup of Chinese roots
- 1 cm (0.39 in) grated ginger root
- 2 garlic cloves chopped in julienne strips
- 1 yellow or green bell pepper that you cut into julienne strips
- 1 ½ cup blanched broccoli florets
- 1 carrot cut into julienne strips
- 1 onion, cut into feathers
- Olive oil
- 1 tbsp sesame seeds
- 4 tbsp soy sauce

Method of preparation

1. Spray the wok with a little extra virgin olive oil, sauté the onions until transparent, and remove. Keep in a large bowl. Drizzle a little oil in the pan again, fry the chili pow-

der for 3 minutes, remove and set aside with the onions.
2. Repeat with the carrots and broccoli separately until they begin to brown and remove them. Drizzle with oil again, sauté ginger and garlic, add the vegetables, stir and combine with honey and soy sauce, until fully mixed.
3. Sprinkle sesame seeds over the sautéed vegetables.

Avocado Cup Bread

This is a very well-known bread among us preppers. It is one that we can make whenever we want with the bunker ingredients.

Ingredients

- ½ cup softened butter
- ¾ tbsp coarse ground pepper
- ¾ ground cinnamon
- ¾ tsp salt
- 1 tsp baking powder
- 1 ½ tbsp baking soda
- 2⅔ cups all-purpose flour
- Egg powder
- 1⅞ cup white sugar
- 1½ mashed ripe avocado
- ¾ buttermilk
- ½ cup raisins
- 1 tbsp orange zest

Method of preparation

1. Preheat the oven to 350°F (175°C). Grease and flour two 9x5-inch loaf pans.
2. Sift together the flour, baking soda, baking powder, salt, cinnamon, and pepper.
3. In a medium bowl, beat together the sugar and butter until light and fluffy. Beat in the eggs one at a time, then add the mashed avocado. Add the dry ingredients alternately with buttermilk until blended. Add the chopped walnuts, raisins, and orange zest and divide the batter evenly between the two loaf pans.
4. Bake in a preheated oven for 1 hour or until a toothpick inserted in the center of the loaf comes out clean. Let the bread cool in the pan for at least 20 minutes before removing it.

CHAPTER 8
DRINKS AND OTHERS

Drinks and others is a special section with recipes designed to fill you up. These are made from the ingredients you have at home.

Sweet Rice Drink

With rice, you can make drinks that have many health benefits. Also, it will have that amazing, sweet touch.

Ingredients

- ¼ cup monk fruit
- 1 cup almond milk
- 3 cups of water
- ½ cup white rice
- ½ tsp cinnamon
- 1 drizzle of vanilla

Method of preparation

1. Put the rice and the water together over a medium heat and wait until there is almost no liquid left.
2. Once you notice that the rice is almost dry, it is cooked, wait until it cools down a little.
3. If you want to try it as a drink, add it to a blender with the rest of the ingredients.
4. However, if you want to get the flavor of condensed rice in this sweet recipe, add milk to the pot while the rice is cooking and some cinnamon sticks—no need to stir it in a mixing bowl. Just serve and add ground cinnamon.
5. Similarly, once your rice drink is on the table, you can add condensed milk if you want to give it more flavor.

Rice Milk With Chocolate

Rice does not only have to taste like rice. With the cocoa powder in the bunker, you can prepare a delicious and nutritious drink.

Ingredients

- ½ cup cocoa
- 1 cup condensed milk
- 1 can of evaporated milk
- ½ cup rice soaked in hot water
- 1 cinnamon piece
- 4 ½ cups of water

Method of preparation

1. Heat water with the cinnamon, bring it to a boil, and add rice; cook over high heat for 10 minutes or until rice is tender.
2. Pour in condensed milk, evaporated milk, and powder ingredients to make the chocolate drink. Stir and continue to simmer for 20 to 25 minutes, until slightly thickened.
3. Heat or cool the rice according to your taste.
4. You can add raisins if you like.
5. Grain rice is rich in folate, a vitamin necessary for cellular reconstruction.
6. You can decorate with strawberries and cinnamon.

Rice Wine

You can enjoy a delicious wine made from rice; here's how to make it:

Ingredients

- 1 ball of yeast for you to prepare wine
- 2 tbsp sticky or glutinous rice

Method of preparation

1. In a small bowl, use a mortar and pestle to crush the yeast balls to make wine. Grind the balls to a fine powder.
2. After crushing the yeast, spread it evenly over the rice. Stir with your hands or a spoon to combine the yeast with the rice.
3. After mixing the yeast and rice, put the rice mixture into one or more airtight containers depending on the size you want to use.
4. Store the rice mixture in a warm place. Put the container in the oven on low heat to stimulate fermentation.
5. After a few days, taste the wine, and you will see that the rice wine accumulates at the bottom of the container. That is rice wine.
6. Let the wine ferment for at least a month.
7. Strain the rice mixture and collect the liquid in a jar or container. Discard excess rice grains and husks.
8. After pouring the rice wine into the container, cover and refrigerate.

Oatmeal

Among all cereals, oatmeal is the most complete and healthy. This is a very low-calorie option that also provides us with vitamins A, B, and E, and various minerals that complement our diet and improve our physical performance. Even so, many people do not know how to eat oatmeal or believe that the only way to eat oatmeal is hot.

Ingredients

- 1 ½ tbsp sugar
- 1 tsp cinnamon powder
- 6 tbsp rolled or flaked oats
- 2 cups of milk

Method of preparation

1. Combine all ingredients except ground cinnamon in a saucepan and cook over medium heat for at least 10 minutes, frequently stirring with a wooden spoon. After that, the flakes should be soft, which indicates that the oatmeal is ready. If not, you should wait until they are soft. The oatmeal should be served hot and sprinkled with a little cinnamon. Nuts or fresh fruits such as strawberries and bananas can be added to this mixture to make the oatmeal more nutritious.

Other ways to eat oatmeal

1. Another easier way to eat oatmeal is as a pick-me-up drink, an excellent choice as a snack in the morning or at least an hour before exercise.
2. In a blender, combine 1 cup of milk, soy or almond milk, 2 tablespoons of oatmeal, sugar, and cinnamon. Allow the mixture to blend well to break down the oats as much as possible. Drink immediately for a refreshing, sweet, and salty taste.
3. If you love fruits and smoothies but want a more natural and healthy option, you can prepare an oat drink as described above, but add fruits like bananas, mangoes, strawberries, or raspberries. It is a great option to eat oatmeal and enjoy all its contributions.
4. If you like cereal and milk, you can add some oatmeal to your bowl to enjoy all its benefits, including its high fiber content, which helps regulate blood cholesterol levels and intestinal transit.
5. If despite these suggestions, you are still looking for other ways to eat oatmeal, this recipe for oatmeal pancakes is sure to blow your mind. all you need is;
    - Cinnamon
    - 1 banana or 1 apple
    - ½ cup oatmeal
    - Egg powder
6. Mix everything in a blender and cook the pancakes in a good non-stick pan. You will be able to enjoy a vibrant and very tasty breakfast.

7. Another great way to eat oatmeal is to add it to the preparation of various dishes. If you like to make desserts, you can add a scoop of oatmeal to your cookies, muffins, or crackers.
8. You can also eat oatmeal by adding it to pickles, such as grated oatmeal, and adding it to salads, vegetable stir-fries, or minced meat recipes such as burgers or meatballs. In this way, in addition to increasing the nutritional capacity of your food, you will obtain a beneficial contribution of fiber.

Hard Candy

It is not a secret that candy is a favorite of many children, so it is a safe bet that the kids at home will be delighted with this easy recipe. Although buying hard candy does not cost much, making hard candy at home can be an interesting option to try simple recipes and get very sweet results.

Ingredients

- Cooking oil
- 1 ½ cup sugar
- 2 cups of water

Method of preparation

1. Before starting to cook the caramel on the fire, you must prepare the mold, which must be suitable for the prepa-

ration of this candy. Choose molds of your preferred size and put them on the table so that you can handle them when it is necessary.

2. It is essential to grease them well before using them, just like when you prepare any other dessert. To do this, you will use a brush or a napkin to dip it in the oil to grease the mold, but do not leave any residue as they will deform our candy. You must make sure that the entire surface is covered with oil so that the caramel does not stick when you unmold it.

3. It is time to prepare the candy. In a pot, pour the water and sugar, heat it over a high fire, and wait for this mixture to change color. When you see that it becomes a caramel color, remove it from the heat and pour it into the container.

4. You can also choose to add vanilla extract or whatever flavor you want to give to the caramel or add color.

5. While the candies are in the molds, they should go in the refrigerator for 15 minutes or leave them in a cool area for a while. After this time, try pouring cold water over the back of the mold to unmold them. If you can't do this, leave the candy to rest for more time until you can unmold it.

VARIOUS RECIPES THAT ARE QUICK TO MAKE

You can make several recipes quickly, depending on what you want to enjoy.

Cold Brew Coffee

In case of a power outage, there is no need to give up coffee, which is essential for many. Even without heating, you can prepare a cup of this energy drink using the cold brew method. You just need a little more time.

Coffee prepared in this way tastes better (but contains all the caffeine), has less acid, and is easier on the stomach.

1. Mix 250 ml of water with 4 tablespoons of ground coffee (or the proportion you prefer) in a glass jar, mix well, cover, and let it rest for about 12 hours. When serving, filter the coffee with filter paper or muslin, and your cup is ready.

Overnight Oatmeal Porridge

Oatmeal is a nutrient-dense grain that has the advantage that, in flake form, no cooking is required: just soak and eat.

To make a basic recipe for one person, combine ½ cup of fine oats, 1 teaspoon of chia seeds, and ½ cup of vegetable drink (or ½ cup of water with 1 tablespoon of vegetable drink or milk powder) and let it sit overnight. Add coconut milk for a delicious porridge.

You can add raisins or other nuts, cocoa, a little maple syrup, coconut sugar, stevia or honey, peanut or almond butter, cinnamon, vanilla, or other spices…

Add more liquid in the morning if it is necessary.

Peanut and Chocolate Cookies

Yummy little cookies that do not require an oven to bake. How to make them:

1. Combine 320 g (11.2 oz) of brown sugar, 120 ml of vegetable drink, 115 g (4 oz) of coconut oil, and 40 g (1.4 oz) of cocoa powder in a saucepan.
2. Bring it to a boil and cook for 1 minute until dissolved.
3. Add a pinch of salt, a teaspoon of vanilla extract, 300 g (10.5 oz) of fine oats, and 150 ml of peanut butter or other nut butter.
4. Mix well and let stand for 20 minutes until the oats absorb the liquid.
5. Form into cookies and put them on a parchment-lined baking sheet for an additional hour—they are ready to eat!

Macaroni Pot of the Forest

The idea behind this dish is to prepare the pasta and sauce together in the same pot. The pasta cooks directly in the sauce, so we save dishes and energy. For 4 people, follow the instructions below:

1. Put 350 grams (12.3 oz) of whole wheat pasta in a pot.
2. Add ½ teaspoon of garlic and onion powder, 1 teaspoon of salt, 1 tablespoon of nutritional yeast, a small can of drained white beans, a handful of dried mushrooms, a teaspoon of thyme or other dried herbs, 2 tablespoons of soy sauce, 350 ml of crushed tomatoes, and 700 ml of water. Bring it to the boil.
3. Cook for about 10–14 minutes until the pasta is ready.
4. Add 2 handfuls of frozen spinach at the end if you have it. If it is necessary, add a little more water and cook a little longer. Taste for flavor and serve.

Couscous With Chickpeas and Pesto

Couscous is probably the most popular grain for emergencies because it requires no cooking. It is a hearty dish for 4 people:

- Heat a cup of water and salt or water with chopped vegetable broth.
- When it starts to boil, add a cup of whole-grain couscous, turn off the heat, mix well, cover and let it stand for about

10 minutes.
- Then add a can of drained chickpeas and 4 tablespoons of pesto and stir to combine.
- If you have some sprouts at home, add a handful and serve.

Mexican Burrito With Beans and Peppers

The container has a shelf life of several months and is perfect for making a simple, quick meal. To make burritos for 4 people:

1. Drain a small can of peppers, 1 can of corn, and 1 can of beans.
2. Cut the peppers into strips. If you have onion, chop the onion and 2 cloves of garlic.
3. Heat 2 tablespoons of oil and sauté the onion and garlic for about 7 minutes in a skillet. Add ½ teaspoon of cayenne, cumin, and smoked paprika (or onion and garlic powder if you do not have fresh) and heat for about 30 seconds.
4. Add the beans, peppers, and corn. Add salt and cook for about 5 minutes, stir and mash the beans a little.
5. Fill the package and serve.
6. You can also use the filling without cooking; just mix the ingredients.

Red Lentil Dahl

Red lentils are beans that require minimal cooking time. If you are short on energy, you can cut the cooking time in half by soaking the lentils for about 8 hours. To make the dahl:

1. Chop 1 onion and 2 cloves of garlic.
2. Add 2 tablespoons of coconut oil to the hot pot. Put the onion into it and sauté for about 5 minutes. If the onion is not in stock, use powdered spices.
3. Then add ½ teaspoon of cumin, ½ teaspoon of coriander powder, 3 teaspoons of curry powder, 1 teaspoon of turmeric, and a pinch of black pepper, then add 200 grams (7 oz) of red lentils.
4. In a few turns in the pot, add 400 ml of crushed tomato, 400 ml of coconut milk, and 500 ml of water and salt.
5. Bring to a boil and cook for about 15 minutes. If you have frozen spinach, cook for a few more minutes.
6. Serve with instant brown rice

Rice Noodles With Coconut Milk and Tofu

It looks like a restaurant dish, but it's an easy plate that you can prepare with pantry ingredients in less than 10 minutes. This dish serves 4 people:

1. Julienne 1/4 cabbage, 1 carrot (if you don't have any, omit), and 1 block of sterilized tofu (if available).

2. Heat 1 tablespoon of coconut oil in a pot, add the vegetables and tofu, 2 tablespoons of soy sauce, and ½ teaspoon of garlic powder. Fry for 5 minutes.
3. Add 2 tablespoons of curry paste (or 4 teaspoons of curry powder), a pinch of ground ginger, 400 ml of coconut milk, 1 liter of water or vegetable stock, salt, and 250 g (8.8 oz) of fine rice flour (e.g., noodles). Cook according to the manufacturer's instructions, about 3-6 minutes.
4. Serve with chili sauce.

Buckwheat Bowl

The good thing about buckwheat is that it can be eaten raw, simply soaked, and it is a very nutritious grain. To prepare a salad for 4 people:

1. Wash 2 cups of buckwheat. Pour into a bowl, cover with 6 cups of water and soak with a tablespoon of apple cider vinegar for 8-12 hours.
2. The drainage is good. You can serve immediately or, if you prefer, add 1 cup of water and a pinch of salt, bring it to a boil and cook until the water is absorbed about 3-5 minutes.
3. Add salt, 4 tablespoons of olive oil, 2 tablespoons of apple cider vinegar, 1 handful of dried cranberries, 1 handful of toasted pistachios, and 2 apple slices to make the salad.
4. Garnish with some green herbs, such as parsley, cilantro, or spinach (if available), mix well, and serve.

Hummus Without a Food Processor

Hummus is a vegetarian staple, and the good news is that it can be made even without electricity or any machine:

1. In a bowl, place 400 grams of drained chickpeas and 2 tablespoons of liquid from the can of chickpeas. Crush them with a fork or potato masher if possible.
2. Add 1 tablespoon of tahini, 1 tablespoon of olive oil, salt, 1 tablespoon of lemon juice, and 1 crushed garlic clove, and stir to combine. Taste and add more seasonings if required.
3. Serve with crackers and whatever vegetables you have on hand.

CONCLUSION

There are thousands of ways in which civilization could come to an end; even now, it may be happening as you read this. Maybe the game over will happen because of a virus launched from somewhere in the world, missiles that may explode in different places, the poles may melt, the world may flood, a great earthquake, or the activation of super volcanoes. In short, the list is long, and the danger is imminent; we are like ants waiting for the stomp in the nest.

Harmony is weak, and we cannot be blind to a reality that is there; work, be kind, feed the family, and do all that you must do, but when it all comes crashing down, you have to be prepared.

Surely before reading this collection, you imagined a prepper to be an obese, alopecic older man wearing a patriotic t-shirt, sitting in a shelter and listening to *The Boss* mumbling incoherently, quite a cliché. However, now anyone can be a prepper, and the need is for everyone to be one.

As a final piece of advice, I suggest you don't tell others outside your nuclear family that you have that bunker because when chaos breaks out, the first house they will go to loot to get food will be yours.

By the time global warming reduces the planet to ashes, we must have a place to survive day-to-day life. You are just in time to start gathering the food, canned goods, preserves, gardens, weapons, medicines, and everything I shared with you throughout this book. I hope you become aware in time, take it seriously and start becoming a prepper like me.